Berlitz®

New York

Front cover: the Brooklyn Bridge and Lower Manhattan

Right: the Statue of Liberty

TOP 10 ATTRACTIONS

Brooklyn Bridge • Stroll across this 19th-century icon *(page 32)*

The Guggenheim • As well known for its architecture as for its paintings *(page 55)*

Statue of Liberty • Welcoming millions to New York *(page 28)*

MOMA • Home to one of the world's best collections of modern art *(page 42)*

imes Square • Get a ringside seat to view the spectacle of
is iconic world landmark *(page 34)*

The Met • A vast and fabulous trove of historical treasures *(page 52)*

reenwich Village • A laid-
ack feel characterizes the
ohemian 'Village' *(page 74)*

American Museum of Natural History • From dinosaurs to planets, it's all here *(page 63)*

Empire State Building • This landmark offers eye-popping views of New York *(page 47)*

ntral Park • Unwind in New York's playground *(page 56)*

A PERFECT DAY

9.00am Breakfast

Enjoy the quintessential breakfast of New Yorkers – bagel, lox and cream cheese – at Katz's Deli on the Lower East Side. After breakfast stroll down Ludlow where you can window shop in the boutiques of this hip neighborhood.

10.15am Step back in time

Just a couple of doors down from Delancy on Orchard Street is the Lower East Side Tenement Museum. Here you can step back in time and learn about the immigrants who originally populated the Lower East Side with a visit to the tenement building built in 1863.

11.15am Walk to Brooklyn

Continue heading south, through Chinatown, to the entrance to the Brooklyn Bridge at the end of Centre Street. Cross the bridge via the walkway to arrive in Brooklyn at the other side of the East River.

12.30pm Pizza perfect

A Brooklyn institution, Grimaldi's pizza (19 Old Fulton Street; exit the bridge via the first stairs) is a must. After lunch wander along Water Street. Grab a hot chocolate or an iced hot chocolate from Jacques Torres before heading to the promenade along the East River in Brooklyn Bridge Park. The views of lower Manhattan are picture-perfect.

IN NEW YORK

2.30pm Old Masters in the afternoon

Take the subway to the Upper East Side. The Frick Collection (1 East 70th Street) is a wonderful, intimate museum, much more manageable than the nearby Met. Built in 1913, the mansion of Henry Frick was designed to accomodate his growing collection of works by artists including Rembrandt, El Greco, Vermeer and Gainsborough.

4.30pm Park life

After the Frick, take a walk through Central Park which is just across 5th Avenue from the Frick. There is an entrance two blocks north at 72nd and Fifth Avenue. Watch the people or even stop to have your portrait done.

5.30pm An early dinner

Many restaurants offer special prix-fixe options for pre-theater particularly in the theater district. Book a month in advance if for the $45 pre-theater dinner at DB Bistro Moderne, Daniel Boulud's French bistro.

8.00pm Broadway

Hit the great white way and enjoy one of the many Broadway or off-Broadway performances.

10.30pm City lights

Top off your day with a perfect panoramic view of the city with all its sparkling lights from Top of the Rock on the 69th floor of the Rockefeller Center.

45

52

37

CONTENTS

Features

70

92

39

GE

INTRODUCTION

First-time visitors to New York usually come with wide eyes and high expectations. And the city generally does not disappoint, even if it frustrates. Few places in the US are as entertaining as New York. No matter what it is you're after, you'll find it: great theater, marvelous museums, luxurious hotels, fascinating history, exciting nightlife, sumptuous dining. The only thing that might be difficult to find here is peace and quiet. But if you stay in a high-rise hotel far above the teeming streets, or venture into the upper reaches of Central Park, or walk out onto the terrace overlooking the Hudson River at the Cloisters, you can find some of that, too.

At first it can all be a little overwhelming: about 13,000 taxis, almost 5,000 city buses, some 6,400 miles of streets, 578 miles of waterfront, 19,000 restaurants, more than 76,000 hotel rooms. However, once you get over the crowded streets, the wailing sirens, the multitude of hawkers, you can start to see that there is more to New York than its tourist attractions and museums. It's a place where people live. Sit on a bench in one of New York's 1,700 parks and watch them go by, or take a stroll through the maze of picturesque Greenwich Village streets.

'The city'

New Yorkers tend to refer to Manhattan as 'the city', even as they identify the other boroughs by name. For addresses, 'New York, New York' means Manhattan.

A City Transformed

If anything characterizes New York today, it's how much the city has raised itself up from the darker days of the 1970s

The Empire State Building

and 1980s. Crime is now at levels New Yorkers have not seen since the 1960s, and the city is generally cleaner and more efficient than it has been for quite a while. As a result, both tourists and business people are flocking here in numbers not seen for years (though there was a perceptible – if only temporary – downturn in room reservations after the appalling events of September 11, 2001). Alongside the flourishing hotel trade, good new (and sometimes not very expensive) restaurants are also opening up right and left, which is great news for visitors and residents alike.

If you want to see an example of how the city can reinvent itself, just look at Times Square. Until the early 1990s, the 'square' was filled with pornographic theaters, adult bookstores, and abandoned buildings. The Port Authority bus terminal was filled with hustlers and touts, and 42nd Street was really not a place one wanted to be after dark. Today Times Square is still choked, but with new, high-profile office buildings and hotels, refurbished Broadway theaters, shiny entertainment complexes, and tens of thousands of tourists. The adult theaters and bookstores have been banished for the most part, and media giants like MTV and Condé Nast have reclaimed the space along with stores such as Toys 'R' Us and

The 9/11 Effect

Every American over a certain age can tell you the story of where they were and what they were doing when President John Kennedy was assassinated on November 22, 1963. Now, every New Yorker can tell you where they were and what they were doing the morning of September 11, 2001 when two terrorist-hijacked planes hit the World Trade Center. The average New Yorker has emerged from the tragedy of September 11 feeling no less rushed and impatient about day-to-day life, but certainly less invincible and far more vulnerable.

Times Square

well-attended attractions including Madame Tussaud's Wax Museum. Some New Yorkers lament that Times Square is now just one big theme park, but the truth is that the area has never been more vibrant.

Not that the story is uniformly positive. The New York area has some of the highest unemployment and poverty rates in the country. The disparity between the rich (who are quite rich indeed) and the poor is greater than ever. Most of the new housing being built in the city will be affordable only to those with the highest incomes. Nevertheless, almost every New York neighborhood, from the South Bronx to Washington Heights, from the upscale Upper East Side to Jackson Heights in Queens, has a good story to tell.

A Heady Mix

It's difficult for mere mortals to live in such a complicated, crowded, and expensive city, so people can easily lose their tempers. But for a place as large and diverse as New York City undoubtedly is, everyone gets along pretty well. The five boroughs – Manhattan, Brooklyn, Queens, the Bronx, and Staten Island – have a total population of around 8.3 million. Brooklyn is the most populous, and Brooklyn and Queens each have more residents than Manhattan. There are more Italians than in Venice, more Irish than in Dublin, and more Jews than in Jerusalem. David Dinkins, a former mayor, was fond of calling New York a 'gorgeous mosaic.'

As a hub for immigration since colonial days, New York has always welcomed the world to sit at its table. Today they still arrive in large numbers, searching for wealth, or happiness, or freedom, or just a job; they come with an entrepreneurial spirit and perhaps nothing else. But they make the mixture richer, by bringing their language and traditions, their likes and dislikes. New York may not be a melting pot, but it is definitely a heady mix.

By the end of their first trip to New York, most visitors are hooked. Nothing is quite as exhilarating as walking the crowded streets of Midtown for the first time, or encountering works of art you've only read about in books, or seeing the Statue of Liberty looming over you from the ferry dock. Or even just strolling through Central Park on a blustery winter afternoon. Whatever you do, don't be intimidated. Walk purposefully, and you'll fit in just fine. Beneath their protective mantle, New Yorkers can sometimes feel just as overwhelmed as tourists. But you'd never know it by looking at them.

Artwork in Lower Manhattan

A BRIEF HISTORY

Giovanni da Verrazano, a Florentine in the service of France, discovered what is now called New York Harbor in 1524, but it would be a hundred years before the first settlers came to the area. Today the entrance to the harbor (the Verrazano Narrows) and the bridge across it are named after him.

New Amsterdam

In 1609, after the Englishman Henry Hudson, working for the Dutch East India Company, sailed up what is now the Hudson River to Albany, excitement finally began to build over the region's possibilities, and in 1624, the new Dutch West India Company sent the first settlers to what is now Lower Manhattan. The following spring the colonists built a small town at the site, calling it New Amsterdam. The first two Dutch governors of the territory, Peter Minuit and Peter Stuyvesant, oversaw the development of a lively trading post. According to a popular city creation myth, it was Peter Minuit who in 1626 purchased the entire island of Manhattan from Native Americans for the equivalent of $24 in beads and cloth, at the site of present-day Bowling Green.

From the beginning, New Amsterdam was the most cosmopolitan center in the New World. The earliest immigrants included Walloons, Scandinavians, Germans, Spaniards, and Portuguese Jews, not to mention black slaves from the Caribbean. In 1643 a priest counted 18 languages spoken in this town of 1,500 inhabitants. An atmosphere of religious tolerance even attracted British dissidents from New England.

In 1653 Governor Peter Stuyvesant built a wall across the expanse of the island (at present-day Wall Street) in an effort to protect the Dutch settlers from the British, who had settled much of the area around New Amsterdam. But the effort was

Painting of George Washington returning to New York (detail)

unnecessary. Unable or unwilling to put up a fight, the Dutch settlers surrendered to an English fleet on September 8, 1664. King Charles II gave the colony to his brother, the Duke of York, and New Amsterdam was rechristened New York.

New York

Although the city again came under Dutch control in 1673 (again without a fight) and was briefly known as New Orange, a treaty the following year returned it to British control. In the 18th century the town grew into a city of 25,000 and life became more comfortable. A city hall and several churches were built, and New York saw the foundation of King's College (today's Columbia University) as well as the creation of its first newspaper, but little of this era remains today. St. Paul's Chapel, built in 1766, is the oldest remaining church in New York. The Morris-Jumel mansion in Harlem also dates from this time.

British control of the colony of New York was a mixed success. Anti-British sentiment started early. In 1735 John Peter Zenger, publisher of the anti-government *New-York Weekly Journal*, was acquitted on charges of slander, an early victory for freedom of the press. (You can read more about the history of this victory at Federal Hall National Memorial in Lower Manhattan.) But the city was split between loyalists to the crown and pro-independence 'patriots.' On June 27, 1775 half the town went to cheer George Washington as he left to take command of the Continental Army in Boston, while the other half were down at the harbor giving a rousing welcome to the English governor, who had just returned from London. Similarly, the New York delegates voted against an early version of the Declaration of Independence.

The New Republic

New York remained a British stronghold throughout the Revolutionary War and only gave up after the final surrender in Virginia in 1781. Two years later England recognized the independence of the American colonies. Washington returned triumphantly to New York and bade farewell to his officers at Fraunces Tavern. He later became the country's first president, when the city was briefly the first capital of the new United States of America. Washington took the oath of office on the balcony of the original Federal Hall (formerly the New York City Hall), then went to pray at St. Paul's Chapel, where you can see his pew.

Although Philadelphia took over as the nation's political capital in 1790, New York remained America's commercial center. In 1800 (the same year Alexander Hamilton built the Grange, which is in today's Harlem), the population had reached 60,000 – twice what it had been ten years earlier.

The city was soon beset with housing shortages and sanitation problems. In the heat of summer, when disease and

Cemetery to park

Many of New York's parks were originally potter's fields, where indigent people were buried. Both Washington Square Park and Bryant Park started out with this function.

epidemics were commonplace, the inhabitants would escape to their 'country' homes in such far-flung places as the village of Greenwich (now Greenwich Village) or the wilderness that became today's Upper East Side. In 1811 the state legislature came to the conclusion that any further growth of New York City must be regulated. The Randel Commission proposed that all new streets should only cross each other at right angles, with streets running east–west and avenues north–south. (Broadway, already an established road leading to the northwest, was exempted.) The plan was immediately adopted, and as a result, everything above 14th Street is now a grid.

Burgeoning Town

When the Erie Canal opened in 1825, linking the Great Lakes to the Hudson River, New York became the ocean gateway for an immense hinterland. Business flourished and shipyards abounded in this major port; housing was still substandard, however, and most residents lived in crowded conditions. In December 1835 a fire destroyed the heart of the business district around Hanover and Pearl streets, including almost all that remained from the Dutch era. But the city recovered quickly from this calamity.

In 1853 the Crystal Palace of the first American World's Fair went up in present-day Bryant Park (behind the New York Public Library). That same year, the state legislature authorized the building of a great public space, Central Park; the architects, Calvert Vaux and Frederick Law Olmsted, were chosen five years later, the same year the Crystal Palace was destroyed by fire.

By 1860, the city's population had reached an unruly 800,000. Governing the city proved difficult, riots occasionally erupted, and, in general, crime was becoming a big problem. Rampant corruption in government was also taking its toll. William Marcy Tweed, who along with his cohorts in the Tammany Hall political organization ran New York City, managed to fleece the city of some $200 million. When 'Boss Tweed' was finally arrested in 1871, the city was in bad shape indeed.

New York nevertheless once again proved its resilience and bounced back. The late 19th century and early 20th witnessed the city's most dramatic growth to date. Many of New York's existing magnificent buildings were built at this time. The construction of the railways that opened up the western lands, the expansion of mines and mills, and the development of the new petroleum and automobile industries were all financed by New York banks. Huge fortunes were made by the Vanderbilts, Rockefellers, Morgans, Carnegies, and Fricks, among others. These tycoons amassed fabulous art collections and funded many of the philanthropic and cultural institutions that make New York what it is today, from the Metropolitan Museum and Metropolitan Opera to the Frick Collection and the Rockefeller Center.

Late 19th-century immigrants

Mass Immigration

During the second half of the 19th century influxes of immigrants crowded into New York in search of a new and better life. The potato famine in Ireland and revolutionary ferment in Central Europe brought the Irish and Germans, who were soon followed by Italians, Poles, and Hungarians. The first important wave of Jews fleeing the pogroms of Russia and Eastern Europe arrived in the 1880s. Over 2 million newcomers landed in the city between 1885 and 1895, welcomed (after 1886) by the Statue of Liberty.

Skyscrapers

By the early 20th century, the development of 'steel skeleton' construction made it possible to build tall. The first genuine skyscraper in New York was the **Flatiron Building**, erected in 1902 and with 22 stories. The **Equitable Building**, however, which appeared on Lower Broadway in 1916, was a monster on an 'H'-shaped ground plan, with 40 floors, and filling an entire block. The walls were perpendicular, without any tiering, thus the whole neighborhood was plunged into shadow. The city was compelled to pass a 'zoning law,' which stipulated that the upper floors of a skyscraper should be tiered to allow light through to the streets below. This resulted in the so-called 'wedding-cake' style of building, examples of which include the **Chrysler** and **Empire State Buildings** (1930 and 1931). Designed by Mies van der Rohe with Philip Johnson, and completed in 1958, the **Seagram Building** on Park Avenue was a simple tower with a straight facade, following the rules of the International Style. It overcame the zoning law by having a plaza at its base, setting the trend for later developments such as Rockefeller Center.

Such a concentration of very tall buildings could never have been built without sturdy foundations, and the billion-year-old gneiss bedrock of Manhattan is as solid as it gets. Its closeness to the surface makes for relatively easy construction (and also explains the shallowness of the subway).

While the middle class moved to west-side neighborhoods near Central Park, the comfortable brownstone houses and mansions of the rich spread up Fifth Avenue and onto the east side. In 1870, construction started on a bridge to connect New York City with Brooklyn, a sizeable city in its own right. The invention of the elevator by Elisha Otis made it possible to construct 'skyscrapers' up to the amazing height of eight or ten stories.

The Flatiron Building

In 1898, New York City (from then on known as Manhattan), Queens, Brooklyn, the Bronx, and Staten Island merged to form Greater New York, with a population of more than 3 million. After London, Greater New York was the world's most populous city.

The early years of the 20th century witnessed further impressive growth. Genuine skyscrapers – including the Flatiron Building (1902) – were built, the first subway line opened (1904), and Manhattan and Brooklyn were finally linked by an under-river subway tunnel (1908). When the business boom finally burst in 1929, bread lines and jobless people became a common sight; a shantytown even sprang up in Central Park. In 1934 a dynamic Italian-born mayor named Fiorello La Guardia fought to introduce an important number of public-welfare measures and civic reform initiatives, which have characterized the city ever since.

Highs and Lows

After World War II, the United Nations set up its headquarters in New York on the banks of the East River (on land donated by the Rockefeller family). The 1950s saw phenomenal growth in the city but also economic downturn. New highways and cheaper cars and houses encouraged city-dwellers to move out to the suburbs. At the same time, in part because of this retreat, portions of the inner city began to decline. Racial tensions also led to riots in Harlem, Bedford-Stuyvesant, and the South Bronx. The city reached a low point in 1975 when New York teetered on the edge of bankruptcy.

After mixed fortunes in the 1980s, the 1990s brought better times. Things started looking up during the mayoralty of David Dinkins, the city's first black mayor, elected in 1989. But most of the improvements were not seen until the voting in of tart-tongued Rudolph Giuliani in 1993. A Republican mayor in a decidedly Democratic city, he brought order to the streets and cleaned up the grime. His 8-year term also accomplished such improvements as a planned subway line on Second Avenue in Manhattan and a rail link to Kennedy Airport in Queens. On September 11, 2001 and its immediate aftermath, Mayor Giuliani took on the unexpected role as the public face of a city in turmoil. He was succeeded in January 2002 by Mayor Michael Bloomberg, owner of the financial media empire that bears his name.

In 2008, the world's attention was once again focused on New York as Wall Street found itself at the center of the global financial crisis.

The New York Stock Exchange

Historical Landmarks

1609 Englishman Henry Hudson is the first European to step on to the island known to the local Algonquin Indians as Mannahatta.
1624 The Dutch West India Company establishes a settlement on the southern tip of Mannahatta (now Battery Park), calling it New Amsterdam.
1664 War between England and Holland. New Amsterdam surrenders and is renamed New York after Charles II's brother, James, Duke of York.
1776 The Revolutionary War begins; the colonies declare independence. British troops occupy New York until 1783.
1785–90 New York is capital of the new United States of America.
1790 The first official census: New York has a population of 33,000.
1830 Irish and German immigrants begin arriving in great numbers.
1835 Part of Manhattan is ravaged by the 'Great Fire.'
1848–9 Political refugees arrive after failure of the German Revolution.
1861–5 American Civil War. New York is on the winning, Yankee side.
1865 Italians, Jews, and Chinese begin arriving in large numbers.
1886 Statue of Liberty, a gift from France, is unveiled.
1892 Ellis Island becomes the entry point for immigrants.
1929 The Wall Street Crash, and the start of the Great Depression.
1931 The Empire State Building opens.
1933–45 Europeans take refuge in New York from Nazi persecution.
1941 The US enters World War II.
1946 The United Nations begins meeting in New York.
1973 The World Trade Center opens.
1975 The city avoids bankruptcy via a loan from federal government.
1990 David Dinkins becomes the city's first African-American mayor.
1993 Rudolph Giuliani voted in as mayor and gets 'tough on crime.'
2000 Crowds flock to revitalized Times Square to see in the Millennium.
2001 Terrorists crash two hijacked planes into the Twin Towers of the World Trade Center. The buildings collapse, killing close to 3,000 people.
2006 Work begins on *Reflecting Absence* memorial at Ground Zero.
2008 Wall Street finds itself at the center of the global financial crisis.
2009 Statue of Liberty reopened to visitors.

WHERE TO GO

While most visitors to New York never leave Manhattan, there is more to the city than its most famous borough. Those who venture to Brooklyn will find a world-class art museum along with parks, gardens, and ethnic neighborhoods. One of the country's great zoos is in the Bronx, near an equally notable attraction, the New York Botanical Garden. In Queens you'll find a top-notch film-making museum. Just getting to Staten Island requires ferry ride right by the Statue of Liberty, and best of all, it's free.

But it's Manhattan that is the focus of most visitors' attentions. Only 13½ miles (22km) long and 2 miles (3.5km) wide, New York's most popular borough is what everyone calls 'the city.' Getting your bearings is remarkably easy thanks to the grid system. Apart from Lower Manhattan, where the thoroughfares twist and turn, and may even be named, all roads running from west to east are called 'streets' and those running from north to south are called 'avenues'. Streets are numbered from south to north and avenues from east to west. Some avenues also have names, such as York Avenue, Lexington Avenue, Park Avenue and Madison Avenue; Sixth Avenue is officially called Avenue of the Americas. Inclusion of 'West' (W) or 'East' (E) in addresses shows whether it lies west or east of Fifth Avenue. There's just one street that doesn't conform to this pattern: Broadway cuts across the island diagonally.

LOWER MANHATTAN

The oldest, most historic part of Manhattan is the Financial District at the tip of the island, roughly the area south of Worth Street, which begins just below Chinatown. Here

Midtown Manhattan from the Empire State Building

you'll find Wall Street, the former site of the World Trade Center, South Street Seaport, and the ferries to Staten Island and the Statue of Liberty. After years of neglect, clubs and bars moved in, making the area worth a visit even after 7pm.

World Trade Center site

For decades, the most visible tourist attraction in Lower Manhattan was the World Trade Center with its huge complex of offices, a hotel, shopping malls, subway stations and the twin towers themselves, crowned by the Windows on the World restaurant and an Observation Deck. When the towers were opened in 1970, they were the tallest buildings in the world.

After September 11, 2001 – when the towers became the target of terrorists causing the deaths of thousands of people from around the world – the **World Trade Center Site** where the complex once stood became a moving memorial, holding as much if not more meaning for visitors as when they came to marvel at the buildings themselves. Today, for many people, a tour of Lower Manhattan starts here at the 16-acre (6-hectare) site. The **viewing wall** surrounds what is now a construction site and allows visitors to see the rebuilding that is underway. The names of the victims of 9/11 are included within the viewing wall; a place

Icon of Hope

Remarkable as it might seem, a huge globe-shaped metal sculpture, *The Sphere* by Fritz Koenig, which stood for more than 30 years in the World Trade Center Plaza, survived the tons of metal and concrete that crashed down upon it on 9/11. In March 2002, it was moved to nearby Battery Park where it stands at the foot of a bed of roses called Hope Garden. On the first anniversary of the attack, an eternal flame was lit here, in memory of the victims.

for quieter contemplation is the nearby St Paul's Chapel (Broadway and Fulton).

Architect Daniel Libeskind drew up a masterplan for the site's redevelopment. On July 4, 2004 the ground was broken on the plan's focal point, the 1,776-ft (541-m) torqued **Freedom Tower** (I World Trade Center) designed by David M.Childs. Acclaimed Spanish architect Santiago Calatrava's beautiful design was chosen for the major, permanent transportation hub. Construction has begun on the memorial, *Reflecting Absence*, which will incorporate the footprints of the twin towers into its design. A good source of information on developments in Lower Manhattan is the Alliance for Downtown New York, Inc. at www.downtownny.com.

September 11 survivor *The Sphere* in Battery Park

Battery Park City

When the World Trade Center was being built in the late 1960s, some 30 million tons of excavated landfill were dumped on adjoining Hudson River docks to create the site of what became, in the 1980s, **Battery Park City**, a collection of high- and low-rise apartment and office buildings and parks. A lovely esplanade lined with parks and gardens stretches along the river from Stuyvesant High School on the north end all the way south to historic Battery Park.

The highlight of the **World Financial Center** is the fine **Winter Garden**, a public atrium ringed by shops, restaurants, and bars. Grab a take-out from a café and join the stockbrokers on one of the benches, or enjoy a more upscale lunch at one of the sit-down restaurants.

A stroll down the promenade is a pleasant way to spend an hour, and also a great place to view the sunset. At the end of the promenade, near the Bowling Green subway station, is the 2 **Museum of Jewish Heritage** (Sun–Tue and Thur 10am–5.45pm, Wed 10am–8pm, Fri 10am–3pm, closed Sat and Jewish holidays; charge; www.mjhnyc.org). Beyond the first floor's interesting multimedia introductory show are galleries about Jewish life and culture; the second floor is devoted to the Holocaust, while the third floor contains exhibits about Judaism today. By focusing on the complexity of Jewish life in the 20th century, the museum is much less depressing than others devoted solely to the Holocaust.

Battery Park City Esplanade

Nearby is **Battery Park**, a leafy expanse at the tip of Manhattan. Most visitors head for **Castle Clinton** – originally the West Battery, a fortification to help protect ships in New York from the English navy, the building dates to 1811. By 1824, its military mission fulfilled, the fort became a concert hall, immigration checkpoint, and even for a while the New York City Aquarium. The National Park Service took over the building in the 1940s and re-named it Castle Clinton. It was re-opened in 1975 as a small museum and the ticket office for ferries to the Statue of Liberty and Ellis Island *(see page 28)*.

Across from Battery Park's northern tip, at the foot of Broadway, is a small triangular patch called **Bowling Green**. It is said that this is where Peter Minuit bought Manhattan from Native Americans for the equivalent of $24 in 1626. Today it is the site of one New York's many Greenmarkets, selling fresh local produce (Tues and Thur 8am–5pm).

Looming over the square is the **Old Customs House**, which is now the home of the **National Museum of the American Indian** (daily 10am–5pm, Thur to 8pm; free; www.nmai.si.edu), a branch of the Smithsonian Institution in Washington, DC (the other Smithsonian branch in NYC is the Cooper-Hewitt on the Upper East Side). The museum celebrates native American culture and showcases a variety of artifacts.

3

Liberty Science Center

From the docks outside the World Financial Center, you can take the New York Waterway Ferry to Colgate Ferry Terminal (Paulus Hook) in New Jersey (every 15 minutes weekdays; www.nywaterway.com) to connect to the Hudson-Bergen Light Rail (Liberty State Park Station) for the Liberty Science Center (Oct–June Mon–Fri 9am–4pm, Sat–Sun until 5pm; July–Sept Mon–Fri 9am–5pm, Sat–Sun until 6pm; charge), which, though not strictly a New York City attraction, is nevertheless a fun place to explore. The exhibitions are designed to appeal to all ages and include a skyscraper area, where visitors can walk along a beam above the exhibition floor and see beams recovered from the World Trade Center. The center also includes an IMAX theater.

Staten Island Ferry

If you're on a tight budget a ride on the free Staten Island Ferry is a great way to get a closer look at the Statue of Liberty. There's not much of interest to visitors on Staten Island, but the 20-minute ferry ride is well worth the trip. Catch the ferry from the end of Battery Park and you'll get stunning views of the Statue of Liberty and the Manhattan skyline, and since the ferry runs 24 hours a day, you can get the same view at night.

Statue of Liberty and Ellis Island

Ferries for the Statue of Liberty and Ellis Island leave from **Battery Park**, calling first at the Statue of Liberty (daily 8.30am–4.30pm in summer, until 3.30pm in winter; departures every 20 mins; www.statuecruises.com).

The **Statue of Liberty** (www.nps.gov.stli) is the most recognized icon of New York City. To access the monument (including lobby, promenade, museum, Fort Wood and the 10th floor pedestal observation area) you will need a Monument Access ticket which is free but must be obtained when you purchase your ferry ticket. There are limited numbers of such passes available each day.

4

Some ten years in the making, the statue was a gift from France in recognition of the friendship between the two countries and has served as a beacon for immigrants arriving in the New World for over 100 years. Creator Frédéric-Auguste Bartholdi's 151-ft- (46-m-) high structure is one of those wild dreams that become reality. Engineering expertise had to be harnessed to art, so Bartholdi called in Gustave Eiffel to work on the complex skeletal framework. Parisian workmen erected the statue in 1884, as bemused Parisians watched her crowned head rise above their rooftops. It was later dismantled and shipped in 214 huge wooden crates for re-assembly on Liberty Island. The statue of *Liberty Enlightening the World* was unveiled by President Cleveland on October 28, 1886.

Once you arrive on Liberty Island you can learn about the history of the statue with 45-min free tours led by Park Rangers. Inside the lobby visitors can view the original torch, the Statue of Liberty exhibit, then proceed to the promenade area for an up close view of the statue and a spectacular view of New York Harbor. Liberty's crown has been re-opened to the public. Visitors can reserve a ticket to climb the 354 steps to the crown when booking their ferry ride. It's a strenuous climb up narrow steps in an enclosed area but rewarded with a great view. The torch remains closed to the public as it has been since 1916.

After the statue, the ferry continues to **Ellis Island**. The island itself was created mostly from landfill from the building of the New York subway system. The museum, which opened in 1990, retraces, through film, audio-visual displays, and exhibitions, the sufferings and joys of some 12 million immigrants who entered the United States through these doors between 1892 and 1954, when overseas consulates took over the screening process. You might find a long lost family member on the Immigrant Wall of Honor. Among notable personalities who made it through Ellis Island were actors Claudette Colbert, Bob Hope, and Edward G. Robinson, composer Irving Berlin, the Von Trapp family of *The Sound of Music* fame, and poet Khalil Gibran.

5

The Statue of Liberty

Fraunces Tavern

Fraunces Tavern

Near the ferry terminal, at 54 Pearl Street (at Broad Street) is **Fraunces Tavern**. First opened for business in 1762 (the original building dated to 1719), this is where George Washington is said to have bid farewell to his officers after the Revolutionary War. The building you see today is mostly a re-creation, built in 1907. Colonial history buffs may appreciate the modest museum upstairs Mon–Sat 12–5pm; charge), which contains documents and period furniture, as well as items such as a lock of Washington's hair, a fragment of one of his teeth, and a shoe that belonged to his wife, Martha; others may opt to dine in the pseudo-colonial atmosphere of the restaurant downstairs together with bankers and brokers (Mon–Sat 11.30am–8.45pm).

The immediate area is absolutely teeming with remnants of old New York. After leaving Fraunces Tavern, if you walk to the right on Pearl Street and turn left at the next corner, you'll come to **Stone Street**, another historic district with a colonial street plan and buildings that were formerly dry goods warehouses and stores. At the other end of Stone Street, after a quick jog to the right, you'll be back on Pearl Street and Hanover Square, which was a wealthy neighborhood during colonial days,

Wall Street

If you continue on Pearl Street, after a couple of blocks you will
6 come to **Wall Street**, perhaps one of the most famous streets in the world, if only for its metaphoric heft. (There was once

an actual wall here, built in 1653 by Dutch governor Peter Stuyvesant to protect New Amsterdam from the encroaching British). Turn left on Wall Street to find several buildings of note. Number 55 Wall Street, which dates to 1842, is one of the oldest buildings on the street. The tallest, at 927ft (283m), is 40 Wall Street. Now known as the **Trump Building**, in 1930 this was briefly the world's tallest before it was eclipsed by the Chrysler Building's spire. The skyscrapers here are closer together than at any other place in the city, the reason why people often refer to the 'canyons' of Lower Manhattan.

At 26 Wall Street (at Nassau), you'll see a large statue of Washington outside **Federal Hall National Memorial** (Mon–Fri 9am–5pm), which was formerly the US Customs building. The original building, demolished in 1812, was the home of the US government for a year when New York was briefly the nation's capital (1785–90); it was also where Washington took the oath as the first president of the US, on April 30, 1789.

Most visitors to the city are more interested in the building across the street, the **New York Stock Exchange**, at 8–18 Broad Street. Interestingly, though Wall Street is synonymous with stock trading, the building's entrance is on the cross street. The NYSE is no longer open to the public for visits or tours.

The Trump Building

The Brooklyn Bridge and Lower Manhattan skyline

Brooklyn Bridge

There are a few other sights of interest to visitors in Lower Manhattan. At the corner of Broadway and Fulton streets is **St Paul's Chapel** and its churchyard. George Washington worshiped here after his inauguration; you can see the pew in which he sat, on the right side of the church as you enter.

A little farther up at 233 Broadway stands the **Woolworth Building**, which reigned as the world's tallest building from 1913 until the Chrysler Building ushered in the skyscraper age in 1930. You can't go upstairs, but take a look at the ornate lobby. Just up Broadway is **New York City Hall**, which is fairly unassuming. And if you're in the mood for a stroll, there is none more scenic or interesting than a trip by foot across the **Brooklyn Bridge**, which opened in 1883 (before then, the only way to Brooklyn was by ferry). The entrance to the pedestrian walkway is on the east side of City Hall Park; take a walk all the way to Brooklyn Heights.

One more detour may be in order for history buffs. At 241 Water Street is the **Seaman's Church Institute**, which has a gallery and ship models. But many are drawn to the area for what is across the street, the **Titanic Memorial Lighthouse**, erected in memory of those lost on the ill-fated ocean liner.

South Street Seaport

A final area of interest in this part of Lower Manhattan is the **South Street Seaport**. This 11-acre (4-hectare), nine-block enclave on the East River at the foot of Fulton Street was once in the middle of the nation's busiest working docks. But its usefulness faded, and the area was turned into a pedestrian mall in the 1960s. In addition to the **South Street Seaport Museum** (Apr–Dec Tue–Sun 10am– 6pm, Jan–Mar Fri–Sun 10am–5pm; charge; www.southstreetseaportmuseum.org), which features mostly nautical memorabilia, there are historic ships moored at **Pier 17**, which you can visit as a part of your museum admission.

8

Pier 17 is a popular spot for summer concerts, shopping, and dining, and the mall has the usual collection of stores. Bypass these unless you're in the mood for shopping, and head upstairs to see the great view of the Brooklyn Bridge. The Fulton Fish Market operated in this location for almost two centuries until 2005 when it was re-located to a new indoor facility in the Bronx. The pre-dawn hours on Fulton Street no longer echo with the shouts of fish-sellers and the squawking of hungry seagulls.

Historic vessels at South Street Seaport

WEST MIDTOWN – THEATER DISTRICT

When visitors think of New York and the Big Apple this intersection of Broadway and Seventh Avenue is usually considered the center of it all. It is also the heart of the Broadway theater district.

Times Square and Broadway

9 Once a seedy, not-so-pleasant place to be, **Times Square** lies at the intersection of Broadway and Seventh Avenue, at the heart of Manhattan's theater district (roughly the area between 42nd and 53rd streets between Sixth and Eighth avenues). Back in the *Midnight Cowboy* years of the early 1970s, it had reached a distinct low point. For a time, the area may have been the 'crossroads of the world,' but it seemed to be so for only the down and out.

Now, it has gotten a new lease on life. Gone are most of the hustlers and prostitutes and pornographic theaters and bookstores; in their place are smart new office buildings, hotels, stores, restaurants, and other attractions that appeal to New Yorkers and tourists alike. One can debate whether this change

Broadway

The name Broadway today is synonymous with theaters, shows, musicals, entertainment, and the glitzy world of the Great White Way, as the section between 40th and 53rd streets was referred to after electric light made its appearance for the first time. Its heyday was in the 1920s and '30s, when there were over 80 theaters on and around Broadway. The most famous section was 42nd Street – so famous in fact that theater owners whose properties were actually on 41st or 43rd Street had passageways constructed through entire blocks of buildings just to be able to boast a 'Forty-Second Street' address.

A ringside seat on the steps in Duffy Square

has made the area blander, but it certainly has revived it. The 'square' is named for the *New York Times*, whose headquarters was once at 1 Times Square (where the ball drops on New Year's Eve). The *Times* has since moved west on 43rd Street to a much larger building, but the name stuck. Other features of the Square include the cylindrical NASDAQ Building at 43rd and Broadway, it's huge electronic display providing up-to-the-minute financial news. At the corner of 44th Street is the Viacom building where MTV's Times Square Studio is located. On the east side of the Square (also at 44th Street), is the new corner studio for *Good Morning America*.

North of Times Square

Across Broadway (between Seventh Avenue and Broadway at 47th Street) you can't miss the glowing red steps in **Duffy Square**, the northern triangle of Times Square. Enjoy a break on the steps as you watch the hustle and bustle of the Times

Carnegie Hall

Financed by the iron and steel magnate Andrew Carnegie, Carnegie Hall was first opened in 1891. Fully refurbished, it is one of the great music venues of the city. If you can't make it to a concert here, at least have a look at the excellent museum.

Square. Under the steps you'll find the TKTS booth which offers discounted tickets to same-day Broadway and off-Broadway plays and musicals

Further north at 1697 Broadway is the Ed Sullivan Theater, where *Late Show with David Letterman* is based. There is an official NYC Information Center for visitors at 810 Seventh Avenue (52nd and 53rd streets). At 135 W. 55th Street (between Sixth and Seventh avenues) is **City Center**. Once a Masonic hall, it is now a theater and dance complex. It's the home of Manhattan Theatre Club. Two blocks north is **Carnegie Hall** (154 W. 57th Street), one of New York's most famous performing arts spaces; the main concert hall (the Isaac Stern Auditorium) is said to have the best acoustics in New York.

West 42nd Street

West of Times Square, on 42nd Street are some of the refurbished theaters and entertainment centers. On the north side of 42nd Street is the **New Victory Theater**, which specializes in children's productions; beyond the **Hilton Theater** is the **E-Walk** entertainment complex, which houses a 13-screen movie theater as well as other amusements. On the south side of 42nd Street is a **Madame Tussaud's Wax Museum**. On the north-east corner of 42nd and Broadway is the **ESPN Zone**, which has a theme restaurant and amusement arcade.

At Eighth Avenue, is the **Port Authority of New York**, the city's main bus station. Once the scariest place in Manhattan, it's still not picturesque, but it is now a thriving and not unpleasant commuter hub, where you can get the bus without being descended on by scores of touts and hustlers. Today the area is dominated by the **New York Times Building**, which was completed in 2007 and ties with the Chrysler Building *(see page 45)* as the third-tallest building in New York.

At the far western end of 42nd Street, Pier 83 is the home to the **Circle Line** that offers tours around Manhattan *(see page 96)*. A little further north, on Pier 86, at 46th Street and Twelfth Avenue, is the popular **Intrepid Sea-Air-Space Museum** (Apr–Sept Mon–Fri 10am–5pm, Sat–Sun 10am–6pm, Oct–Mar Tue– Sun 10am–5pm; charge). The *Intrepid*, a decommissioned US Navy aircraft carrier, is packed with exhibits on sea exploration and warfare, space travel, and aviation. Two other major components of the museum are the submarine USS *Growler* and a Concorde.

10

Hot dog stalls are ubiquitous

CENTRAL MIDTOWN

A wealth of cultural and shopping attractions are found in this area of midtown. From art (MoMA) to literature (New York Public Library) to the department stores of Fifth Avenue.

Bryant Park

East of Times Square on 42nd Street, between Sixth and Fifth avenues, are the green and leafy expanses of **Bryant Park**, another great New

Diamond District

West 47th is New York's Diamond District, an area dominated by mostly Orthodox Jewish diamond dealers; believe it or not, a majority of the diamonds that pass through New York find their way to this unassuming street. While this may be a good place to shop for diamonds, it's questionable as to whether or not you'll find any real bargains at the jewelry or discount electronics stores.

York restoration project of the early 1990s. The present French-style layout of the park dates from the Great Depression, but by the 1980s it had become a no-man's land of drug dealers night and day. Now it is one of midtown's most pleasant oases, where office workers gather in the summer months for lunch or just to relax. Next to the park is the **New York Public Library**, a grand Beaux-Arts-style building that dates to 1911; two handsome, famous and much-photographed stone lions, Patience and Fortitude, flag its Fifth Avenue entrance. One of the largest research libraries in the world, the structure houses several million books, almost as many manuscripts, and several vast reading rooms. The main reading room, which was re-opened in 1999 after a major restoration, has been modernized and brought back to its original grandeur. Changing exhibitions are regularly mounted in the library's exhibition halls.

Just north of Bryant Park at 1133 Avenue of the Americas at 43rd Street, the **International Center of Photography** (Tue–Sun 10am–6pm, Fri 10am–8pm, closed Mon; charge) houses a collection of over 100,000 images covering the entire history of photography, in the heart of midtown.

Rockefeller Center

The centerpiece of central Manhattan, covering 22 acres (9 hectares) between Fifth and Sixth avenues, from 47th to 51st streets, is **Rockefeller Center**. The buildings in this complex are linked by underground walkways and concourses, which are themselves filled with shops, a post office, and restaurants. Columbia University purchased the site in 1811 when it was still farmland. In 1928, John D. Rockefeller, a founder of the Standard Oil Company, asked the university for a lease on the site to raise a commercial complex. Built mostly between 1931 and 1940, Rockefeller Center attracts thousands of office-workers, visitors, and shoppers daily. Much of the area, including the ice-skating rink, has undergone major renovation.

From Fifth Avenue you enter via the **Channel Gardens**, a sloping walkway divided by fountains and flowerbeds between the British and French buildings, which end at the sunken plaza and its famous ice rink and gilded **statue of Prometheus**. This is also where the giant Christmas tree is placed (right behind Prometheus). If you have time, wander around and admire some of the Art Deco details.

The ice rink and statue of Prometheus at Rockefeller Center

Radio City Music Hall

Nowadays, the **GE Building** (30 Rockefeller Plaza, the largest building in the complex) is better known as the headquarters for the NBC television network and the *Today Show* – the glassed-in studio is across the street from the building's southeast corner (at 49th Street). Its observation deck is called **Top of the Rock** (entrance on W. 50th Street; daily 8am–midnight; charge; www.topoftherocknyc.com), and offers visitors an unparalleled and unobstructed 360-degree view of the city from the 70th floor. The elevator to the top features a transparent ceiling so that visitors can view their rapid ascent all the way up the elevator chute. A light show and projected images add to the fun of the ride.

Also at this corner is the **NBC Experience**, a combination attraction and store for merchandise festooned with the logo of the network and some of its television shows. You can also buy tickets here for the NBC Studio Tour, whose high price doesn't seem to detract from its popularity (Mon–Thur tours every 30 mins 8.30am–4.30pm, Fri–Sat tours every 15 mins 9.30pm–5.30pm, Sunday tours every 15 mins 9.30am–4.30pm).

Radio City Music Hall (corner of Sixth Avenue and 50th Street) is one of the largest theaters in the world, with a seating capacity of around 6,000. This restored Art Deco masterpiece is the popular location for seasonal theme shows, including the dazzling Christmas Spectacular; it's also the home of the ever-popular Rockettes. Stage Door Tours can be arranged on tel: (212) 307 7171, or at www.radiocity.com.

Fifth Avenue

At the turn of the 20th century, **Fifth Avenue** was the location of one of the largest and most opulent mansions in New York. After World War I, a number of fashionable and expensive stores opened for business here. You'll still find Saks Fifth Avenue (50th Street), Henri Bendel (55th and 56th streets), Tiffany's (57th Street), and Bergdorf Goodman (57th Street), though most of the trendiest designers now have their boutiques on Madison Avenue. The gaudiest addition to Fifth Avenue has without a doubt been Donald Trump's **Trump Tower** (56th and 57th streets), where a 'wall' of water slides down rose marble set between gleaming brass escalator rails.

13 **St Patrick's Cathedral**, on Fifth Avenue (50th and 51st), was the tallest building in the vicinity when it was built between 1858 and 1879. Today, however, it appears somewhat dwarfed by the skyscrapers of Rockefeller Center and the apartment building next door, though the juxtaposition of its soft gray granite and the surrounding glass creates a stunning image. Seat of the Archdiocese of New York City, the church is the focal point of the Irish parade on St Patrick's Day.

At the corner of Fifth Avenue and 59th Street, busy **Grand Army Plaza** marks the division between Fifth

St Patrick's Cathedral reflected

Avenue's shopping area and the residential section, which is lined with exclusive apartment buildings and a few remaining mansions. This is the place to hire a horse-drawn carriage for a ride round Central Park *(see page 56)*. It's also the site of two of New York's most famous hotels, the **Plaza** and the **Pierre** (at East 61st Street). Across from the plaza is the General Motors Building and the giant toy store, **FAO Schwarz**. A distinctive 32-ft (10-m) glass cube in front of the General Motors Building marks the entrance to the massive subterranean **Apple Store** (767 Fifth Avenue), where you can browse among the iPods, iMacs, and other Apple products 365 days a year, 24 hours a day.

The glass-cube entrance to the Apple Store

Museum of Modern Art

One of midtown's most important cultural centers is the **Museum of Modern Art**, or MoMA (Wed–Mon 10.30am–5.30pm, Fri until 8pm; charge; www.moma.org), located on 53rd Street between Fifth and Sixth avenues. An extensive rebuilding program, with additions designed by architect Yoshio Taniguchi, has recently doubled the museum's exhibition space. 14

Devoted to works of art created after 1880, roughly from the Impressionists on, the collection includes such masterpieces as Dalí's *The*

Persistence of Memory, Van Gogh's *The Starry Night*, Rousseau's *Sleeping Gypsy*, Wyeth's *Christina's World* and Warhol's *Gold Marilyn Monroe*, plus a number of Monet's *Water Lilies*, as well as important works by Picasso, Jackson Pollock, Mark Rothko and Chuck Close. Modern sculpture is not ignored, and there are examples of everything from Marcel Duchamp's bicycle wheel as sculpture to huge installations by contemporary artists. The modern sculpture garden remains a distinctive element of the new MoMA.

Inside MoMA

The flagship MoMA design store, a great place to buy artistically designed house-hold wares, is located within the museum; a second store is across the street at 44 West 53rd Street. There is a third shop in Soho (81 Spring Street).

Due west of MoMA, at 45 West 53rd Street, is the **American Folk Art Museum** (Tue–Sun 10.30am–5.30pm, Fri to 7.30pm; charge). Celebrating the 'extraordinary ccomplishments of ordinary people,' the museum has exhibits ranging from 18th- and 19th-century paintings, to quilts, to contemporary sculpture.

EAST MIDTOWN

In this area you will spend much of your time looking up at major architectural landmarks, including the ceiling of Grand Central and the Chrysler Building.

Madison and Park Avenues

The streets east of Fifth Avenue have several places of interest to visitors. The **Sony Wonder Technology Lab** in the Sony Building at Madison Avenue and 56th is aimed at the younger set; parents can shop at Sony Style downstairs. The 57-story tower of the **New York Palace Hotel** (East 50th and 51st) incorporates the historic Villard Houses, which date to 1882. Take a walk through the grand lobby if you are in the area.

A Park Avenue landmark is the **Waldorf-Astoria Hotel**, which takes up the entire block between Park and Lexington from 49th to 50th. It has been host to world leaders since 1931. Nearby, the bronze-and-glass **Seagram Building**, on Park Avenue between 52nd and 53rd, is the only New York building designed by Mies van der Rohe; it's also the home of the famous Four Seasons restaurant (52nd Street). Across the street, at 390 Park Avenue, is the 24-story **Lever House**. Built in 1952 it was one of the first glass-walled office buildings in the States.

Grand Central and the Chrysler Building

After a complete restoration and renovation project in the late 1990s, **Grand Central Terminal** (at 42nd between Park and Lexington) has been returned to its former splendor. Completed in 1913, the building is a great Beaux-Arts masterpiece. Inside, 31 rail lines arrive on the upper level, 17 on the lower. The central concourse, vast but also light, airy, and harmonious under a blue-green, star-sprinkled ceiling 12 stories high, is invaded every afternoon from 4 to 6pm by

15

Grand Central sculpture

hundreds of thousands of suburban commuters catching their trains home to points north of Manhattan. If you enter from the Vanderbilt Avenue side, look across the lobby to see the grand staircase, only recently added to the building. Inside the station are restaurants, shops, and, on the lower level, the famous **Oyster Bar & Restaurant**, a favorite for power-lunchers. Free tours are offered twice a week, on Wednesdays at 12.30pm by the Municipal Arts Society (meet at the information booth on the Grand Concourse; tel: 212-935 3960), and on Fridays by the Grand Central Partnership (meet at 12.30pm in the sculpture court at 120 Park Avenue, located at the southwest corner of East 42nd Street and Park Avenue directly across from Grand Central Terminal; tel: 212-883 2420).

The Chrysler Building

Across Lexington Avenue on 42nd Street stands the most beautiful skyscraper of all, the **Chrysler Building**, a silvery Art-Deco needle completed in 1930. A recent cleaning has made the top of the building gleam; a major interior renovation should give it life through the next century. For a few months it was the tallest structure in the world, but it was rapidly surpassed by the Empire State Building *(see page 45)*. The stylized eagle heads on the upper corners were modeled on the Chrysler automobile's 1929 radiator cap.

The Daily News Building lobby

At the corner of Second Avenue, even more fine Art-Deco architecture distinguishes the former **Daily News Building**; the lobby, with its huge revolving globe, is well worth a look. The paper moved west of Penn Station a few years ago. Also well worth a look is the **Ford Foundation** headquarters (320 East 42nd Street); offices open onto a spacious interior court with trees – New York's first office-building atrium. It's another of the city's fine public spaces.

United Nations

The eastern end of 42nd Street used to be a warren of tenements and slaughterhouses, but thanks to John D. Rockefeller, Jr., it is now the home of the **United Nations**. A team of 11 architects, including Wallace K. Harrison, Le Corbusier, and Oscar Niemeyer, designed the buildings, which were completed in the early 1950s. The Secretariat is housed in the glass-and-marble upright structure, while the General Assembly meets in the lower building with the slightly concave roof. The flags of all the member nations flutter from the flagpoles along First Avenue.

17

When the General Assembly is not in session, visitors from around the world take daily multilingual tours of the General Assembly Hall and Council Chambers, the sculptures in the grounds overlooking the East River and Queens, and informative documentary exhibits. A highlight is the meditation room adorned with stained-glass windows by Marc Chagall

SOUTH MIDTOWN

Empire State Building

Though the **Empire State Building** (corner of Fifth Avenue and 34th Street; daily 8am–2am; charge; www.esbnyc.com) no longer holds the title of tallest building in the world, it is otherwise everything a skyscraper should be: 102 stories; 60,000 tons of steel; 3,500 miles (5,632km) of telephone wires and cables; 60 miles (97km) of pipes; a total volume of 1¼ million cubic yards (1 million cubic meters); 1,860 steps, and of course, its towering height – 1,453ft (443m), including the lightning rod (overall, half as tall again as the Eiffel Tower). 18

Opened in 1931 in the depths of the Great Depression, the building took just two years to complete. The 86th-floor Observation Deck provides stunning views of New York. On the outside terrace you can see much of Manhattan, including Central Park, and on a clear day you can see ships 40 miles (64km) away. You can also visit the 102nd floor observatory (additional charge), from which King Kong swatted wasp-like attacking airplanes.

The Empire State Building

Back on earth, you can go west along 34th Street to visit **Macy's** (Sixth and Seventh avenues), New York's most famous and largest department store, and also the

Taking in the view from the Empire State's observation deck

Manhattan Mall. Nearby, at Seventh Avenue and 33rd Street, is **Madison Square Garden**, renowned for boxing matches and rock concerts. In addition to being home to the New York Knicks (basketball) and the Rangers (ice hockey), it is also used as a conference center. The Garden seats 20,000 people and its adjacent theater can take an additional 5,000. Under Madison Square Garden is Pennsylvania Station (usually referred to as Penn Station), the railway terminal for New Jersey and Long Island commuters and for Amtrak. Across Eighth Avenue is the **General Post Office**, which was a twin to the old Penn Station, torn down in the late 1960s to make room for Madison Square Garden. The post office building is poised to become a new, even grander Penn Station in the near future.

If you are in New York for a trade show, chances are that you'll head for the **Jacob K. Javits Convention Center**, the city's largest exhibition center, a striking building on Eleventh

Avenue between 34th and 37th streets. Designed by I. M. Pei, the center was named for New York state's long-time Republican senator.

To the east of the Empire State Building, at 36th and Madison in Murray Hill, is another prominent landmark: the **Morgan Library**, which has re-opened after a major expansion and renovation. J. Pierpont Morgan's personal collection of rare books and manuscripts includes three Gutenberg Bibles and Florentine sculpture and art. Often overlooked by tourists, it's a quiet place, which is one of its pleasures.

UPPER EAST SIDE – THE MUSEUM MILE

Home to many of New York's famous museums, the Upper East Side starts at 59th Street, at the corner of Central Park. Beyond the east 60s, much of this area is residential, and includes some of Manhattan's most expensive real estate. This is where you'll find the former residence of Jacqueline Onassis and the current homes of many of the city's society doyennes.

CityPass

One way to see several of Manhattan's top attractions and to save some money at the same time is to buy a CityPass, which gives you admission to six leading attractions (the Empire State Building Observation Deck, the Guggenheim Museum, the Museum of Modern Art, the Metropolitan Museum of Art, the American Museum of Natural History, and Circle Line Sightseeing Cruises or Statue of Liberty and Ellis Island), for only $79 – considerably less than the total for individual full admission prices. You can buy the pass, which can be used for nine consecutive days, at any of the participating attractions; it should enable you to avoid most ticket lines.

Most of the Upper East Side's museums are located along the so-called 'Museum Mile' from 82nd to 104th streets. But there are a few exceptions. One is the **Mount Vernon Hotel Museum and Garden**, at 421 East 61st Street (First and York avenues; Tue–Sun 11am–4pm; closed Aug; charge; www.mvhm.org). This Federal-style house, which dates from 1799, is an interesting period piece for those with time and interest, featuring 19th-century furnishings and decorative arts.

Frick Collection

A few other major museums are just off the Museum Mile proper. (19) The **Frick Collection** at 70th Street and Fifth Avenue (Tue–Sat 10am–6pm, Sun 11am–5pm, closed Mon; charge; www.frick.org) is situated in the former mansion of coal and steel baron Henry Clay Frick, who put together one of the finest private collections of art in the US (mostly European paintings

The Frick mansion and gardens

and sculpture). Upon the death of Frick's widow in 1931, their home, which was designed by Thomas Hastings, and the art therein were donated to the city of New York as a museum; it opened in 1935 after a reconstruction designed by John Russell Pope. Visitors to the collection have the pleasure of seeing not only beautiful works of art but also the mansion and its gardens, much as they were when the Fricks lived there. And it's a rare and wonderful experience. In addition to three Vermeers (including *Mistress and Maid*), the museum holds fine works by Holbein *(Sir Thomas More* and *Thomas Cromwell)*, El Greco *(St. Jerome)*, Bellini *(St. Francis in Ecstasy)*, Boucher, Titian, Goya, Whistler, Rembrandt, and Velázquez; exquisite European furniture; and one of the largest collections of small bronze sculptures in the world.

Asia Society

The attractive red-granite building on the northeast corner of Park Avenue and 70th Street is the headquarters of the Asia Society. The society mounts regular, imaginative exhibitions of ancient and modern Asian and Pacific art assembled from private collections, as well as from its own permanent collection. It's open Tues–Sun 11am–6pm, Fri until 9pm (except Jul–Aug); admission fee.

Whitney Museum

Located on Madison Avenue (at 75th Street) is the excellent **Whitney Museum of American Art** (Wed–Thur, Sat–Sun 11am–6pm, Fri 1–9pm; charge; www.whitney.org), a unique gallery for several reasons. Firstly, it was founded by an artist (Gertrude Vanderbilt Whitney), though admittedly an artist from one of New York's wealthiest families. Second, it is one of the few museums that is dedicated solely to American art and that seeks out works from alternative media, such as film and video. The Whitney seems to go out of its way to court

controversy with its spring Biennial exhibition. But by focusing its collection on contemporary American artists (both those of Ms. Whitney and those of today), it has also gone a long way toward changing attitudes about the diversity and strength of American art. The permanent collection includes works by such artists as Andy Warhol, Alexander Calder, Georgia O'Keefe, Jackson Pollock, Jasper Johns, and Mark Rothko. Curators continue to build and show works by living artists.

Metropolitan Museum of Art

21 Museum Mile begins at the **Metropolitan Museum of Art**, located at 82nd Street and Fifth Avenue (Tue–Thur, Sun 9.30am–5.15pm, Fri–Sat 9.30am–8.45pm; charge; www.metmuseum.org). Monumentally huge, the 'Met,' as it is affectionately known, is a repository for all things cultural, from Egyptian mummies to Roman bronzes to Chinese pot-

The Metropolitan Museum of Art

tery to wonderful Impressionist paintings. Founded in 1870, the institution owns over 2 million items, though only around a quarter of the total collection is on display at any one time in its nearly 250 rooms. The stunning new Greek and Roman galleries are worth a closer look since a redesign and reinstallation of the galleries was completed in 2007. More than 5,300 works of classical art are now on show; many of them have not been on public display in decades. Also recently refurbished are the galleries devoted to Asian art. Children love the Egyptian galleries (the best such collection in the US), especially the Temple of Dendur, which sits in its own room with a view of Central Park. But they also enjoy the Arms and Armor halls and the African galleries.

Egyptian exhibit at the Met

Don't miss the American Wing, particularly the tranquil Garden Court. You'll find stained-glass windows, the facade of a Wall Street bank, fountains, and sculptures, along with plants and benches to sit on to quietly contemplate the surroundings. On all sides are period rooms and other galleries that show off the Met's fine holdings in American art. Among the famous paintings are Emanuel Leutze's *Washington Crossing the Delaware*, Albert Bierstadt's *The Rocky Mountains*, as well as notable works by Winslow Homer.

European paintings, sculpture, and decorative arts before 1800 include Botticelli's *Last Communion of St. Jerome*, Giovanni di Paolo's *Adoration of the Magi*, Rembrandt's *Self-Portrait, 1660*, and works by Bellini, Ingres, El Greco, Holbein, Goya, and virtually any other famous

Special exhibitions

Visitors should look out for special exhibitions at the Met; no additional ticket or admission fee is required to see them.

painter you can name. Similarly, the collection of 19th-century European paintings and sculptures, including works by such luminaries as Van Gogh, Monet, Renoir, and Degas, is stellar. The Robert Lehman Collection, at the west end of the main floor, comprises fine Old Masters and Italian Renaissance paintings, including several period rooms recreated from Lehman's home. The Michael C. Rockefeller Wing houses a very good collection of primitive art.

The Lila Acheson Wallace Wing, devoted to modern art, remains one of the most popular sections of the Met. It features paintings, sculptures, and decorative arts from Europe and America, including Picasso's *Gertrude Stein* and works by major modern artists including Jackson Pollock, Willem de Kooning, Edward Hopper, Georgia O'Keefe, Diego Rivera, Frank Stella, and Chuck Close.

Modern sculpture is on view in the roof garden overlooking Central Park, where there is a café in the summer. On top of all this, the Met has one of the best art bookstores in the US.

Neue Galerie

Four blocks north of the Met (1048 Fifth Avenue at 86th Street) is the **Neue Galerie** (Thur–Mon 11am–6pm; charge; www.neuegalerie.com), a fine museum that specializes in German and Austrian art, featuring works by Klimt and various Bauhaus exponents. It is housed in an elegant mansion built in 1914 for the industrialist William Starr Miller by Carrère and Hastings, architects of the New York Public Library; the building was once occupied by society doyenne, Mrs Cornelius Vanderbilt III. The Café Sabarsky inside *(see page 113)* is recommended too.

Guggenheim Museum

At 89th Street is the **Solomon R. Guggenheim Museum** 22 (Sun–Wed, Fri 10am–5.45pm, Sat 10am–7.45pm, closed Thur; charge; www.guggenheim.org). The building, which was designed by Frank Lloyd Wright and opened in 1959, is now a New York landmark. The concrete exterior was comprehensively restored for the museum's 50th anniversary in 2009. The museum's most famous feature is perhaps not its paintings but the continuous spiral ramp that connects the building's six storeys.

The permanent collection, built on Guggenheim's original private collection of contemporary paintings, includes works by such artists as Brancusi, Klee, Chagall, Picasso, Miró, Calder, and Kandinsky. The Justin K. Thannhauser collection, in the annex, contains paintings by Renoir, Monet, Cézanne, Van Gogh, Gauguin, and Degas. The museum's collection is actually now spread somewhat thinly among its various branches in such disparate places as Bilbao, Las Vegas, Venice, and Berlin.

Just across 89th Street is the **National Academy Museum** (Wed–Thur noon–5pm, Fri– Sun 11am–6pm; charge; www. nationalacademy.org), whose collection focuses on American art of the 19th and early 20th centuries.

The Guggenheim

And More Museums...

Nearby, at 91st Street, is the **Cooper-Hewitt National Design Museum** (Mon–Fri 10am–5pm, Sat 10am–6pm, Sun noon–6pm; charge; www.cooperhewitt.org). A branch of the Smithsonian Institution, the Cooper-Hewitt is more of a research institution than a museum. Though its collections are available to anyone by appointment, most of the vast holdings of furniture, wall-coverings, textiles, prints, drawings, and miscellaneous objects are not on display. But if there is a special exhibit that interests you, a visit to the mansion and its lovely gardens can be a treat.

At 92nd Street, the **Jewish Museum** (Thur–Tue 11am–5.45pm, Fri until 4pm, closed Wed and Jewish holidays; charge, free Sat; www.jewishmuseum.org), housed in a gothic mansion, is an important cultural and historical museum. It holds an extensive collection of Judaica and exhibits the work of Jewish artists.

The **Museum of the City of New York** (Tue–Sun 10am–5pm; charge; www.mcny.org) is located at 103rd Street. This treasury of materials documenting New York City's history also includes a superb toy collection. The last institution on Museum Mile is **El Museo del Barrio** (Wed–Sun 11am–5pm; charge; www.elmuseo.org), at 104th Street. Americans of Hispanic origin are scattered in many parts of the city's five boroughs, but El Barrio – the Quarter – in East (or Spanish) Harlem was the first predominantly Puerto Rican district. The museum is devoted to Latin American culture and art.

CENTRAL PARK

The heart (some say the lungs) of Manhattan is **Central Park**, located between 59th and 110th streets and Fifth and Eighth avenues. This vast green space is half a mile wide and 2½ miles long (0.8km x 4km) and is one of the main places

Relaxing in Central Park, the lungs of Manhattan

where New Yorkers go to play. On summer weekends, residents (and visitors) come by the thousands to play ball, skate, stroll, picnic, or listen to a concert. But the park is busy all week long and all year long. The park's designers were Frederick Law Olmsted and Calvert Vaux, and the project, which began in 1858, took almost 20 years to complete. Creating a usable public space from a huge, sparse, and rocky landscape was a remarkable achievement for the time and revolutionized landscape architecture. Amazingly, almost everything in the park, from the Great Lawn to the lakes, to the meadows and forest in the northern end, was constructed. The park is now partially supported, administered, and overseen by the Central Park Conservancy.

There is always something going on in the park, from a concert to a rally to a bicycle race. To learn more about the park you can take a walking tour. The Central Park Conservancy sponsors free tours year-round, rain or shine.

No reservations required (tel: 212-360-2726 Tues–Sat for information). The more active will be interested in ball fields, tennis courts, and other sporting opportunities. Since most of the park's roads are closed at weekends, strolling, biking, and skating are popular pastimes.

The Dairy

You might want to drop in at the Dairy (mid-Park at 65th Street; Tue–Sun 10am–5pm), the Central Park visitors' center. The attractive Victorian Gothic structure was actually built as a dairy in 1870 in order to provide fresh milk to families. Today it displays a permanent exhibit on the park's history and design and provides visitors with brochures and information.

Park Highlights

Highlights in the southern end of the park include **Wollman Rink** (mid-Park at 63rd Street), which is used for ice-skating in the winter. A children's amusement park takes over during the summer months. There's another skating rink in the northern end of the park, Lasker Rink (between W. 106th and 108th streets), which is transformed into a very popular swimming pool in the summer.

23 Closer to Fifth Avenue is the **Central Park Wildlife Center**, including the **Tisch Children's Zoo** (in between is the George Delacorte Musical Clock, which chimes the hours with musical animals). The highlights of the Wildlife Center include the sea-lion pool and polar bear house. The zoo has both a petting zoo and the 'Enchanted Forest.' The admission charge to the Wildlife Center includes entrance to the zoo, and both are open daily.

Another favorite in the southeast corner of the park is the historic **Carousel**, located mid-Park at 64th Street. It dates from 1908 and used to stand in a Coney Island amusement park. You can still ride it, weather permitting (Apr–Dec daily; Jan–Mar weekends only).

On the park's west side, near 66th Street, is **Tavern on the Green**, one of two restaurants in Central Park (the other being at Loeb Boathouse). The setting is dazzling, and the gardens, illuminated at night by thousands of lanterns and lights, make a wonderful spot for a celebration, which won't come cheap. Nearby is the **Sheep Meadow**, one of New York's favorite places for playing frisbee and for sunbathing in the summer; it's also a great place for a picnic. The sheep that used to graze here were originally housed in the Tavern on the Green building.

Right in the middle of the park, beginning at 66th Street, is the **Literary Walk**, lined with statues of writers you will, for the most part, recognize. The path leads up to the Mall, where there is a band shell, and ends at the **Bethesda Terrace and Fountain**, one of the park's best-known spots. On the lake here is the Loeb Boathouse, where there is a café in addition to a good (though also fairly expensive) restaurant open year-round. You can rent a boat or a bike near here in the summer.

To the east is the **Conservatory Water**, a model-boat pond; at its northern end (at 74th Street) sits Central Park's most beloved sculpture, a bronze grouping of favorite characters from Lewis Carroll's *Alice's Adventures in Wonderland*. To

With Alice and the Mad Hatter

the west is **Strawberry Fields**, a memorial to John Lennon, who on 8 December 1980 was killed outside the nearby Dakota apartment building at 72nd Street and Central Park West. North of this (at 80th Street) is the **Delacorte Theatre**, where you can see free plays during the summer. And in the center of the park is **Belvedere Castle**, which affords some excellent views; inside is a nature center and the park's weather station.

From the Castle, you'll be able to see the central part of the park, which features the **Great Lawn**, a huge expanse popular with sun-worshipers. On the east side is the Metropolitan Museum of Art *(see page 54)*, and just to the south **Cleopatra's Needle** (at 81st Street), a 3,600-year-old obelisk (not connected to Cleopatra) that was a gift from Egypt in the 19th century.

Walkers in the park

North of here are several other notable features. The jogging path around the **Jacqueline Kennedy Onassis Reservoir** (mid-Park, north of 86th Street) is a favorite with runners. The **North Meadow** (mid-Park, at 96th Street) is another open expanse, often the site of free concerts. At 104th Street is the **Conservatory Garden**, a group of formal gardens that are popular for weddings. And at the northern end of the park on the east side is the **Harlem Meer**, a lake.

UPPER WEST SIDE

The Time Warner Center at Columbus Circle

Beginning at **Columbus Circle**, where Broadway and Eighth Avenue (thereafter renamed Central Park West) converge, the Upper West Side stretches north to around Columbia University (about 110th Street); its western boundary is the Hudson River and Riverside Park; its eastern boundary is Central Park. Columbus Circle has been reinvigorated by the towering new Time Warner Center overlooking Central Park; the center includes the headquarters of Time Warner (including CNN), a retail complex, the Mandarin Oriental Hotel, a collection of restaurants including some of the biggest names in fine dining (including Thomas Keller's Per Se), and the new home of Jazz @ Lincoln Center.

At 2 Columbus Circle is the **Museum of Arts and Design** (Wed–Sun 11am–6pm, Thur to 9pm; charge; www.madmuseum.org) and its collection of everything from teapots to antique quilts and rocking chairs to contemporary Native American pottery.

Lincoln Center

25

The cultural epicenter of the Upper West Side is the **Lincoln Center for the Performing Arts**, which is bounded by 62nd and 66th streets (on the south and north), Amsterdam (the continuation of Tenth Avenue) on the west, and Columbus (the continuation of Ninth Avenue) on the east. The Center covers an

The Dakota

area of 16 acres (7 hectares). The central plaza, a vast esplanade surrounding a fountain, acts as the focal point for the three main buildings. Built in 1960, the whole space is in the midst of a vast modernisation program

In the center is the **Metropolitan Opera House** (the other 'Met'), home to the Metropolitan Opera and the American Ballet Theater; it was designed by Wallace K. Harrison and completed in 1966 and can hold nearly 4,000 people. Two Chagall murals adorning the central lobby can be seen from the outside. To the left of the Met is the **David H. Koch Theater**, home of the New York City Ballet and the New York City Opera. Designed by architect Philip Johnson and built in 1964, it has a simple, stately facade complemented by a red-and-gold auditorium studded with crystal; the notoriously bad acoustics were recently upgraded through the installation of a modern sound system. To the right of the Met, opposite the David H. Koch Theater, is **Avery Fisher Hall**, completed in 1962, which is primarily used for music concerts.

Just behind Avery Fisher Hall, to the right of the Met, you can make out the outline of **Vivian Beaumont Theater**; the structure was designed by Skidmore, Owings & Merrill, but the two theaters inside were designed by Eero Saarinen.

Farther back, but connected to Lincoln Center by a footbridge over West 65th Street, is the Juilliard School, one of the world's outstanding music conservatories.

Farther north are several interesting things to take a look at. The Beaux-Arts Ansonia building, at 2109 Broadway

(73rd and 74th streets), is a notable apartment building. A little farther west, at the corner of 72nd and Central Park West, is the **Dakota**, which dates to 1884; it has been home to such rich and famous residents as Lauren Bacall, John Lennon and Yoko Ono, and Roberta Flack.

A few blocks farther north, between 76th and 77th streets, is the **New-York Historical Society** (Tue–Sun 10am–6pm, Fri until 8pm; charge; www.nyhistory.org), the oldest museum in New York (the second-oldest in the US). In addition to documents and artifacts of historical interest, the Society's collection includes American fine and decorative arts.

Natural History Museum

The huge building on Central Park West at 79th Street is the **American Museum of Natural History** (daily 10am–5.45pm; charge; www.amnh.org), another of New York's

26

Dinosaurs at the Natural History Museum

The Hayden Planetarium

oldest museums, dating to 1869. Once a pretty stuffy place full of old dinosaur bones and dusty taxidermy displays, much of the museum has been renovated and reinvented over the past few years; crowds are drawn to the **Hayden Planetarium**, the centerpiece of the Frederick Phineas and Sandra Priest Rose Center for Earth and Space. The impressive Hall of Planet Earth is part of this newest section.

With tens of millions of specimens and artifacts, the museum is a repository for knowledge of virtually any aspect of earth's natural history and development. The creaking dioramas are still there and now seem quaint. But the more recently refurbished parts of the museum, including the Fossil Halls (covering everything from dinosaurs to mammals) and the Hall of Biodiversity (which includes a life-size recreation of a rainforest), have the most up-to-the-minute scientific information and wonderful state-of-the-art exhibitions.

Don't miss the full-size model of a blue whale, the Star of India (the largest sapphire ever discovered), and the Barosaurus in the Theodore Roosevelt Rotunda on Central Park West (it's the tallest free-standing dinosaur exhibit in the world). Tours of the collection's highlights are given regularly throughout the day. The museum also has an IMAX theater.

Columbia University Area

Many visitors are surprised to find one of the largest neo-Gothic cathedrals in the world in New York City. The **Episcopal Cathedral Church of St John the Divine**, at Amsterdam Avenue and 112th Street (daily 7am–6pm), was begun in 1892 and is yet to be completed. You can see the scaffolding around the unfinished spire. The church is well known for its jazz and choral music series, in addition to its rotating art exhibits.

Beyond the cathedral, at 116th and Broadway, lies the campus of **Columbia University**. Founded in 1754 as King's College, Columbia is New York City's representative in the Ivy League. A private university, its schools of law and journalism and the teacher's college are widely recognized for their excellence. (The School of Journalism administers the Pulitzer Prizes each year.) The campus itself is striking. Right across Broadway stands Barnard College, Columbia University's affiliated women's college.

Not far away, in Riverside Park at West 122nd Street, is **Grant's Tomb**, the mausoleum of General Ulysses S. Grant, Commander-in-Chief of the Union Army in the Civil War and US President from 1869 to 1877, and his wife, Julia Dent Grant. After the war, the general settled in New York City and worked on Wall Street and died here in July 1885. Administered by the National Park Service, the mausoleum, which is the biggest in the US, contains a museum (daily 9am–5pm, closed Federal holidays; free), which is devoted to Grant's life.

27

Columbia University students

HARLEM AND NORTH MANHATTAN

Harlem is currently undergoing a cultural and economic renaissance, and has witnessed rapid gentrification in recent times. Considered a major African-American cultural, spiritual and business center, Harlem is a vital and varied community with rich, poor and middle-income sections, historical landmarks and attractive homes.

A popular way to see Harlem is on one of the hop-on-hop-off double-decker bus tours or a specialized tour that often includes lunch and a gospel music performance; tours that include a Sunday church service are especially popular. For more information, *see page 124*.

Harlem begins north of Central Park at 110th Street and extends to 178th Street, bounded on the west by Morningside Heights and Washington Heights and on the north and east by the Harlem River, which connects the Hudson and East rivers. The neighborhood's commercial center is 125th Street, where you'll find the historic **Apollo Theater** (253 West 125th Street).

Historic District

Founded by Dutch settlers, Harlem remained a village for a long time. As immigrants moved into the Lower East Side, many middle-class families moved north to Harlem. The

Harlem's Churches

Central Harlem is known for its beautiful churches. The Abyssinian Baptist Church at 132 West 138th Street was founded in 1808; its current Harlem home dates to 1923. Also in the area are the Mother AME Zion Church, at 146 West 137th Street, which is the oldest black congregation in New York. St Philip's Episcopal Church is a striking neo-Gothic building at 204 West 134th Street.

influx of black families started around 1900 and reached its height around 1920, when the area became a cultural hub and home to prominent artists and writers associated with the Harlem Renaissance. Historic row houses of this period are preserved in the **St Nicholas Historic District** between Adam Clayton Powell, Jr. Boulevard and Frederick Douglass Boulevard on 138th and 139th streets.

Historic Harlem

There are several prominent cultural institutions in the area. 28 **The Studio Museum in Harlem**, 144 West 125th Street, at Lenox Avenue (Wed–Fri noon– 6pm, Sat 10am–6pm, Sun noon–6pm; charge; www.studiomuseum.org) is dedicated to African-American, Caribbean, and contemporary and traditional African art. At Malcolm X Boulevard and 135th Street, the **Schomburg Center for Research in Black Culture** (Mon–Wed noon–8pm, Thur-Fri 11am–6pm, Sat 10am–5pm), a branch of the New York Public Library and an art museum, possesses one of the world's most important collections covering black history and African-American culture.

North of Harlem is the **Hamilton Grange National Memorial**, which was the early 19th-century home of Founding Father Alexander Hamilton. The house, having undergone a move to St Nicholas Park and restoration, is due to reopen in 2010. The surrounding area, roughly between St Nicholas and

Eating in Harlem

If you yearn for something to eat in Harlem, there are many good choices. The place that says Harlem for most people is Sylvia's (328 Lenox Avenue, at 127th Street, tel: 212-996 0660), where you can sample typical South Carolina fare; its Sunday gospel brunch is especially popular. Another eatery is Charles' Southern Style Kitchen (2841 Frederick Douglass Boulevard, between 151st and 152nd streets, tel: 212-926 4313).

Edgecombe avenues and 143rd to 155th streets, was once Hamilton's farm. It is now known as **Hamilton Heights** and is home to a historic area that includes the Sugar Hill row houses. The stately restored **Morris-Jumel Mansion** and gardens (1765) at 65 Jumel Terrace (near 162nd street) exhibits period furniture (Wed–Sun 10am–4pm; charge; www.morrisjumel.org).

The 1908 Beaux-Arts style **Audubon Terrace** complex, on Broadway between 155th and 156th streets, is home to two cultural institutions. Firstly, there's the **American Academy of Arts and Letters** (tel: 212-368 5900), which has seasonal exhibitions but is otherwise not open to the public. Then there's the **Hispanic Society of America**, which has a permanent collection that includes rare books and manuscripts and works by Goya and El Greco. Entrance to the society's library and museum is free to the public (library and museum Tue–Sat 10am–4.30pm; Sun 1–4pm museum only).

Washington Heights

Above Harlem, Manhattan narrows to a little sliver made up of **Washington Heights** and Inwood. Both are primarily residential neighborhoods, but there are a couple of interesting attractions. Washington Heights is predominantly a Dominican neighborhood; long known as a drug-seller's haven, it is beginning to clean up its act.

The Cloisters

Beyond Washington Heights is **Fort Tryon Park**, 66 acres (26 hectares) of landscaped and terraced hills, which begins at 190th Street. From the subway stop (A line) here, it's possible to walk through the park or take a city bus to **The Cloisters** (Tue–Sun 9.30am–4.45pm, until 5.15pm in summer; charge). Part of the Metropolitan Museum (your admission to the Met also gives you same-day admission here), this branch is devoted to Medieval art and architecture. It is built around parts of several actual cloisters and other medieval structures. The views of the Hudson River from the outdoor terraces are breathtaking, and the gardens provide a great place to sit in reflective solitude.

29

Housed within The Cloisters are several genuine masterpieces, including the wood sculpture *Enthroned Virgin and Child*, a set of 'nine heroes' tapestries, a 12th-century carved ivory cross, and the museum's most popular holding, a set of tapestries depicting the *Hunt for the Unicorn*.

Not far away is the **Dyckman Farmhouse Museum** at 4881 Broadway (Wed–Sat 11am–4pm, Sun noon–4pm; charge), the only remaining Dutch colonial farmhouse in Manhattan. If you're in the neighborhood, it's worth a detour.

Medieval Cloisters

OTHER NEIGHBORHOODS

The Lower East Side

At the turn of the 20th century, the Lower East Side of Manhattan was the most densely populated place in the US, home to around half a million Russian and Eastern European Jewish immigrants. The remnants of the old Jewish neighborhood are located on the northeast side of Chinatown, beyond Hester Street, the site of the Jewish market at the end of the 19th century. Follow Hester Street east and then walk north along **Orchard Street**, and you'll see a shadow of the market's heyday mixed in with hip eateries and new clubs. Dormant on the Jewish Sabbath from Friday evening to Saturday at sunset, the area springs back to life on Sunday.

The Lower East Side Tenement Museum

In this New World ghetto, the cornerstone of the economy was the 'needle trade.' Working conditions and pay were appalling. Those who didn't enter the trade often worked as peddlers or pushcart vendors, selling produce or cheap clothing in the markets on Hester Street and Orchard Street. The **Lower East Side Tenement Museum** at 97 Orchard Street offers an introduction to this area. The 19th-century tenement can be seen by guided

30

tour only, and visitors view restored apartments of immigrant families in the tenement at different historical periods. Tours start from the Visitor Center, across the road at 108 Orchard Street (daily 10am–6pm, last tour at 5pm; charge; advance ticket purchase recommended; www.tenement.org).

Exotic Chinatown produce

The Bowery

The Bowery is located on the eastern border of the Lower East Side. Once notorious as New York City's skid row, the Bowery and surrounding neighborhoods are being gentrified, with luxury condominium buildings going up at a rapid pace. The upscale Whole Foods Market at the corner of Bowery and Houston is always busy and a good place to take a break and grab a snack from a large selection of prepared foods. On the Bowery across from Prince Street is the **New Museum**, opened in 2007 (Wed–Sun noon–6pm, also 6–9pm Thur and Fri; charge). This is the first new art museum constructed from the ground up in downtown Manhattan and the only one in the city devoted exclusively to contemporary art.

Chinatown

Of all the ethnic neighborhoods that were established on New York's Lower East Side, it's the Chinese enclave that has continued to thrive. The narrow shops sell ivory and jade jewelry as well as bootleg designer watches and the usual souvenirs; grocers display exotic Chinese produce; and the area's innumerable restaurants feature a huge range of regional specialties. Well over 200,000 people live in bustling **Chinatown**, a loosely defined area embracing Canal Street, Chatham Square, and Mott Street. The earliest Chinese arrivals came to America in the 19th century, during the California Gold Rush and the period of railway construction; most immigrants today come from the Fujian province in southern China. At 215 Centre Street is the new, greatly expanded home of the **Museum of Chinese in America** (Mon–Fri 11am–5pm, Thur until 9pm, Sat–Sun 10am-5pm; charge; www.mocanyc.org) In addition to cultural programs and exhibitions the museum conducts walking tours of the neighbourhood. Near Chatham Square, at the corner of Division Street and Bowery, stands a 1983 bronze statue of Confucius, and south of the square, a few steps down St. James Place, are some of New York's oldest monuments, barely a dozen tombstones, the remnants of the **Shearith Israel Cemetery**, founded here in 1656 by New York's first immigrants, Spanish and Portuguese Jews.

Cops on the beat in Little Italy

Little Italy

'Little' is certainly the operative word here, as this area has now been largely subsumed by Chinatown. The stretch of Mulberry Street from Canal to Grand is still home to several Italian restaurants and expensive coffee bars. In the summer, especially on weekends, it's a pleasant place to stroll, buy a souvenir, and have a plate of pasta and a glass of house wine al fresco. There are still some good bakeries and grocers here, though some of them, too, are now Chinese. The district is at its liveliest during the ten-day Feast of San Gennaro in early September *(see page 98)*. But if you find yourself in the neighborhood, you might want to take a stroll over to the old **Police Headquarters** at the corner of Centre and Grand streets; this is the building in which Theodore Roosevelt served as New York City's police commissioner. The inhabitants are now the tenants of the luxury condominiums created in the late 1980s.

The colours of Little Italy

Soho and Tribeca

Soho (South of Houston) is the area bound by Houston Street, Broadway, Canal Street, and the Hudson River. It has become the Village's chic southern neighbor, with expensive cafes, restaurants, art galleries, and shops selling the very latest in fashion and housewares. Its history has followed the pattern of Greenwich Village. Artists who couldn't afford the rents after the Village's commercialization moved south to the derelict lofts and warehouse floors of the then industrial district. The most successful were able to install kitchens, bathrooms, and comfortable interiors, while others made do with bare walls and floors for the sake of ample space and light. Now the same lofts sell in the multi-million-dollar range.

The main things to do here are to browse in the galleries, stop and relax at the many outdoor cafés and restaurants, and shop. Broadway is the most mainstream shopping street. A fun place for kids is the the **Scholastic Store**, 557 Broadway (Mon–Sat 10am–7pm, Sun noon–6pm). In addition to books, toys, DVDs, videos and games, it has creative displays featuring *Clifford The Big Red Dog*, *Harry Potter*, *Dora the Explorer*, *Captain Underpants*, *The Magic School Bus*, and other Scholastic favorites. Events, activities, and storytellings are held nearly every day.

West Broadway is the liveliest of the Soho streets. Here you'll find the choicest shops and galleries, though there are selections of both on the side streets and now all over the area.

After Soho became too expensive, the dealers moved in, and the artists moved out, many heading southwest to the derelict warehouses of the **Tribeca** (Triangle Below Canal) neighborhood, which in its turn has inevitably seen the opening of art galleries, upscale restaurants, and trendy boutiques. As the rents began to soar, many of the artists migrated to Williamsburg in Brooklyn; even some of the art dealers have moved out.

De Niro's Tribeca

Tribeca's high-priced loft-style real estate is home to many high profile New Yorkers. But perhaps the district's most ardent resident-supporter is actor Robert De Niro. He opened his restaurant Tribeca Grill, which is still going strong, and instituted the Tribeca Film Festival.

Greenwich Village

'The Village,' as **Greenwich Village** is usually called, has been separate, casual, and very different from the rest of the city ever since its beginnings. In colonial times it really was a distinct village called Greenwich, which became a neighborhood of conservative Georgian brick houses and carriage barns in back-alley mews. A few of these houses remain, mostly on **Bedford Street** and the streets around it, but conservative the Village isn't. It got its bohemian reputation after World War I, when artists and writers who found cheap lodgings, inexpensive restaurants, and speakeasies scattered throughout the Village, decided to call it home. Later, the Village became the center for New York's gay community, which to some degree has moved north to Chelsea.

The Village is roughly the area from 14th Street down to Houston and west of Broadway. The area's heart is **Washington Square Park**, the de facto campus quadrangle for **New York University**, which controls much of the real estate east of Sixth Avenue and south of 14th Street to Houston. The park's famous arch was designed by architect Stanford White and erected in 1889 to mark the centenary of George Washington's inauguration as president.

32

Washington Square Park

Hidden away behind these buildings surrounding Washington Square are two private lanes that used to lead to the stables belonging to the area's elite: **Washington Mews**, one block up Fifth Avenue from the park on your right, and **MacDougal Alley**, just a few steps up MacDougal Street from the northwest corner of the square.

Bleecker Street with its craft and curio shops, antique stores, cafés, and tiny restaurants has long been the main

Gay Liberation statue in Christopher Park

shopping strip of the neighborhood. The area's highest concentration of gay and lesbian businesses and bars is still found on **Christopher Street**, west of Seventh Avenue South. The **Stonewall**, at 53 Christopher Street, stands on the site of the original Stonewall Inn, which was the site of the riots in 1969 that led to the modern gay rights movement. You may wish to make at least two trips to the Village – by day to shop and see the sights, and at night to catch the atmosphere, have dinner, and hit one of the jazz clubs or bars.

East Village

A separate community, the **East Village** extends east from Broadway to Avenue D and the East River. Much less affluent than Greenwich Village to the west, this neighborhood is nevertheless seeing signs of gentrification. You'll find small boutiques, restaurants, and interesting shops that can't afford the other downtown rents. If there is any real bohemian spirit left in Manhattan, it may be here. A walk down St Mark's Place or Avenue A, the liveliest streets, can almost take you back to the 1960s; stop for a rest and some great people-watching in Tomkins Square.

On Lafayette Street, just to the south of Cooper Square, stands the building that once housed the first public library of New York. Nowadays it's the seat of **The Public Theater**, which actually contains several theaters and is the home of the New York Shakespeare Festival. Joe's Pub, off the main lobby, is a celebrated venue for live music and performance. Nearby is the Great Hall of the Cooper Union, the center of the free university established by Peter Cooper in 1859.

Those interested in historic buildings might stop by **St Mark's-in-the-Bowery**, built in 1799 on the very spot where the Stuyvesant family chapel once stood (at 10th Street at Second Avenue). It is now a charming church with some noteworthy stained-glass windows – and an extremely lively congregation, often hosting music or dance performances.

Village Voices

Since the Art Nouveau period, Greenwich Village has been one big 'village of genius' and home of the artistic avant-garde. The radical paper *Masses*, whose contributors included Maxim Gorki, Bertrand Russell, and John Reed, had its offices here. In 1914, Gertrude Vanderbilt Whitney opened a gallery and provided a platform for contemporary artists, much of whose work was highly controversial. In 1916, members of the Playwrights' Theater settled on MacDougal Street and soon achieved fame – Eugene O'Neill among them.

After World War II the Bohemian image of 'the Village' persisted. In the 1950s, the beatnik movement flowered (Jack Kerouac and Allen Ginsberg); in the 1960s and early '70s the area was home to hippies and anti-Vietnam war activists (Abbie Hoffman and Jerry Rubin).

Steps up to the High Line

Meatpacking District and Chelsea

The northwest corner of Greenwich Village from West 14th Street to Gansevoort Street is a designated historic district of cobbled streets and warehouses. Home to a meat market during the last century, the area has now been transformed, with plenty of trendy boutiques, restaurants, bars, clubs and hotels.

The **High Line** (daily 7am–10pm; www.thehighline.org), a major new public park, opened its first section (from Gaansevoort Street to West 20th Street between 10th and 11th avenues) in 2009. The elevated railroad tracks that were originally constructed in the 1930s to lift freight trains off the streets of Manhattan are now a beautifully landscaped walkway. There are multiple entrances and exits. When all sections are open it will be a 1.5-mile long park through the far west side neighbourhoods.

33

The neighborhood between 14th and 39th streets west of Sixth Avenue is also thriving after many years of decline. It's also one of the trendiest gay neighborhoods in Manhattan. Stroll up Eighth Avenue, where you'll find gay bars and boutiques, as well as restaurants catering to all types. The **Joyce Theater**, at 19th Street, is one of the city's main modern dance venues. On 23rd Street, between Seventh and Eighth avenues, the Chelsea Hotel, originally a cooperative building, now houses artists permanently and other guests nightly. In far west Chelsea, the **Chelsea Piers** sports and entertainment complex is along the Hudson River from 17th to 23rd streets.

Seventh Avenue is quieter, but you'll still find many restaurants and stores. Loehmann's, on Seventh Avenue at 16th Street, is a prime source for discounted designer clothing. Sixth Avenue from 18th to 23rd streets was once known as the 'Ladies Mile.' For many years, the massive storefronts stood derelict; now they are inhabited by such retailers as Old Navy and Bed, Bath, and Beyond.

Chelsea has long superseded Soho as the place for **contemporary art**. There are close to 200 galleries on the far west side between Tenth and Twelfth avenues.

EXCURSIONS TO THE OUTER BOROUGHS

Brooklyn

Brooklyn, which actually has a larger population than Manhattan, is one of America's largest urban centers. It's well worth a trip over the East River. **Brooklyn Heights**, the neighborhood closest to Manhattan, is easy to reach. Take subway numbers 2 or 3 to Clark Street, or cross the Brooklyn Bridge on foot from the east side of City Hall Park *(see page 32)*; the view is unparalleled.

Rising above the East River, the Heights is an attractive area of 19th-century brownstones and picturesque streets, long popular with writers and artists. The **Promenade** (three blocks down Clark Street from the bridge), is an esplanade with an impressive view, including both the Manhattan skyline and the Statue of Liberty. Late afternoon is a good time to go, when the towers of Lower Manhattan start to glow in the light of the setting sun. At the end of the Promenade, walk south along shady Hicks Street, in a quarter that has changed little since 1860.

If you are interested in subways and how they are run, then a trip to the **New York Transit Museum** (Tue–Fri 10am–4pm, Sat–Sun noon–5pm; charge) is in order. Housed in an authentic 1930s subway station at the corner of Boerum Place and Schermerhorn Street, the museum has a great variety of exhibits, many with interactive components. They also have an annex museum in Grand Central Terminal *(see page 44)*.

34 The **Brooklyn Museum** (200 Eastern Parkway; Wed–Fri 10am–5pm, Sat–Sun 11am–6pm; charge; www.brooklynmuseum.org) is the second-largest museum in New York, with exceptional collections of Egyptian, Asian, Persian, and pre-Columbian art. The permanent collection includes more than 1.5 million objects, and the African art collection is one of the largest and most important in the United States. In 2004 the museum unveiled a new glass entrance pavilion, which celebrates the historic Beaux-Arts façade. The redesigned public plaza welcomes visitors to one of the premier art institutions in the world. Take the 2 or 3 subway to Eastern Parkway-Brooklyn Museum.

Brooklyn Botanic Garden

Adjacent to the museum is the **Brooklyn Botanic Garden**. Not to be confused with the larger New York Botanical Garden in the Bronx *(see page 80)*, it's nevertheless a peaceful place to stroll. Nearby is **Prospect Park**, a 526-

acre (212-hectare) urban oasis designed by Frederick Law Olmsted and Calvert Vaux (who designed Central Park). A combined visit to the museum, botanic garden, and park is a nice way to spend an unhurried day.

Stalking Siberian tiger at the Bronx Zoo

The Bronx

For a while now, the **Bronx** has had a reputation for crime and urban decay. While there are certainly parts of the Bronx where this is still true, visitors who haven't been here lately will be surprised. Several attractions make it worth a special trip to New York's only borough on the US mainland.

35

One such attraction is the **Bronx Zoo** (Mon–Fri 10am–5pm; weekends until 5.30pm; Nov–Mar 10am–4.30pm; charge, reduced in winter, free Wed). At its most inviting from May through October, when all of the sections are open, the zoo has over 4,000 animals of almost 600 species. At the Congo Gorilla Forest (separate fee) you get to meet the zoo's gorillas up close. Though they are behind glass, there is still a lot of interaction with the crowd. Other popular exhibits and attractions are Wild Asia monorail (where you can see tigers; separate fee), JungleWorld, the World of Birds, Children's Zoo (separate fee), and the World of Darkness (nocturnal animals), and, in the summer, the Butterfly Garden (separate fee).

To get to the zoo, take the 2 or 5 subway to East Tremont/West Farms Square. When you exit at street level, walk straight ahead (follow train uptown) on Boston Road 2½ blocks to the zoo's Asia gate entrance (Gate A). Alternatively, you can take Metro North from Grand Central to Fordham station, then catch the BX9 bus to the Southern Boulevard Entrance. You can also take the BXM11 Express Bus from Midtown, which runs express up Madison Avenue. The Bronx Zoo is the first stop after 99th Street.

Adjacent to the zoo is the 250-acre (100-hectare) **New York Botanical Garden** (Tue–Sun 10am–6pm, in the winter until 5pm only; charge). Highlights include several specialty gardens, an orchid collection, a 40-acre (16-hectare) uncut, almost virgin forest, and the Enid A. Haupt Conservatory. Children will enjoy learning about plants and nature in the adventure garden. The visitor center includes a shop, café, and visitor orientation area. To get there, take Metro North from Grand Central to the New York Botanical Garden stop; alternatively, you can take the D or 4 subway to Bedford Park Boulevard, but this requires a long walk or additional bus ride.

Yankee tours

Baseball fans may be interested to know that you can take a 60-min tour of the new Yankee Stadium in Bronx during baseball season (May–September) but only on certain days when the team is not playing at home. You must make an advance ticket reservation through Ticketmaster (tel: 877-469-9849) or online at <http://mlb.mlb.com/nyy/ballpark/stadium_tours>.

Queens

The most diverse borough of the five that make up New York, Queens has several attractions that will interest visitors. During the silent movie era, Queens was the equivalent of today's Hollywood – the center of the motion-picture industry – and movies and TV shows are still made at the Kaufman Astoria Studios here. Located in the studio complex, on 35th Avenue at 36th Street in Astoria, the **American Museum of the Moving Image** (Wed–Thur 11am–5pm, Fri 11am–8pm, Sat–Sun 11am–6.30pm; charge) celebrates this early movie history and explores the art, technique, and technology of film, television, and digital media, examining their impact on society. To reach the museum, take the R subway to Steinway Street or the N to Broadway (Astoria) and walk.

In Long Island City, just across from midtown Manhattan, is the **P.S. 1 Contemporary Art Center** (22–25 Jackson Avenue at 46th Street; Thur–Mon noon–6pm; charge), the largest contemporary art museum in New York and well worth a visit. To get there, take the E or V subway to 23rd Street/Ely Avenue or the 7 to 45th Road/Courthouse Square.

Also in Long Island City is the **Noguchi Museum** (9-01 33rd Road, at Vernon Boulevard; Wed–Fri 10am–5pm, Sat–Sun 11am–6pm; charge), created by Japanese-American sculptor Isamu Noguchi. The former photo-engraving plant serves as an interesting backdrop for a comprehensive collection of the artist's works in stone, metal, wood, and clay.

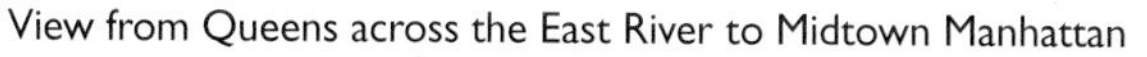

View from Queens across the East River to Midtown Manhattan

Black & Gold®

WHAT TO DO

SHOPPING

If you can't afford to buy (and in the stores on Madison Avenue that may well be the case), you can at least window-shop. Virtually anything is available in Manhattan for a price, which is sometimes, though certainly not always, a bargain.

When and Where to Shop

If you are looking for inexpensive New York souvenirs, avoid Midtown and the areas around major tourist attractions (such as the Empire State Building). Instead, try 14th Street, particularly between Fifth and Sixth Avenues, as well as Chinatown, especially the north side of Canal and the blocks on either side of Mulberry. Greenwich Village can still be an interesting place to shop; browse the quirky smaller stores along Bleecker Street (antique shops are concentrated on the western stretch, beyond Christopher Street). Soho, a major weekend destination for area shoppers, is the home of fine art galleries and designer-clothing and home-furnishings stores. There are also quite a few boutique clothing stores in Chelsea. And, of course, don't forget the East Village.

The reliable standard shopping neighborhoods have always been Fifth Avenue above 50th Street (for decades very chic but now increasingly more predictable and loaded with chain and theme stores) and Madison Avenue from Midtown to the Upper East Side (home to some very luxurious, high-end shops). Manhattan's newest shopping destination is the **Time Warner Center** overlooking Central Park, where more than 40 high-end retailers take up four floors of prime retail space at the base of the building on Columbus Circle.

What to Buy

Art and Antiques. Art galleries and antiques shops are found throughout the city. The largest concentrations are along East 57th Street and up Madison Avenue to 84th Street. A movement away from Soho, where there are still some galleries, has led to a boom in new galleries in west Chelsea. There are some good antique stores on Bleecker Street, west of Christopher Street in Greenwich Village. One institution worth visiting for its wide range of choices is the **Manhattan Art and Antiques Center** (1050 Second Avenue at 56th Street), which boasts some 100 galleries selling ceramics, crystal, and assorted bric-a-brac.

Chelsea's the place to go for good flea markets, both open-air and enclosed. Try the **Antiques Garage** at 112 West 25th Street (Sixth and Seventh avenues), where you will find over 100 vendors. It is open on weekends all year-round. Not too far away and also open every Saturday and Sunday is **Hell's Kitchen Flea Market** (39th Street between Ninth and Tenth avenues) with even more vendors including manyselling vintage clothing and jewelry.

Clothing. You really can find bargains among the prodigious array of clothes in the department stores, especially during end-of-season sales. But it would be a shame to limit your search to the bigger stores. Head to Madison Avenue above 60th Street for high-fashion boutiques, to Soho (expensive) and the East Village (less expensive) for more daring designs, to Fifth Avenue for reliable luxury labels, and to Chelsea (particularly along Eighth Avenue) for club-wear. The best place for discount designer clothing is **Century 21** (22 Cortlandt Street, between Broadway

Macy's, the giant

Macy's, established in New York City in 1858, is the world's largest store, at 2.1 million sq ft (189,000 sq m). It stocks more than 500,000 items.

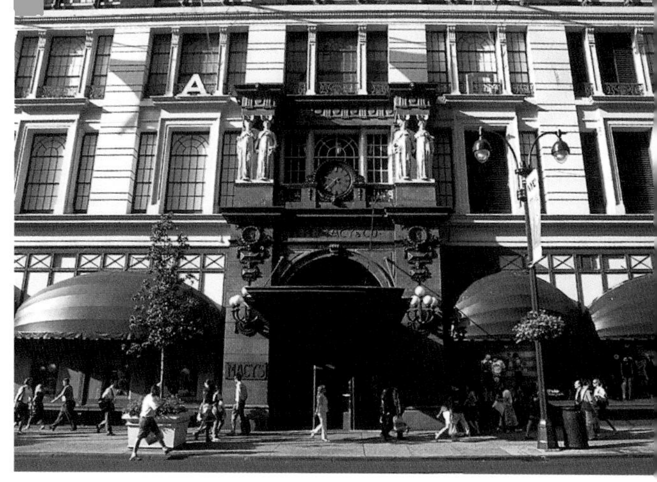

Macy's, the world's largest department store

and Church); almost everything starts at half price, and sometimes there are real bargains.

Computers and Electronics. Approach the so-called 'discount' electronics stores to be found all over Midtown with a critical eye; sales techniques can be high-pressure and the prices are not always as good as you might think. Many of the dealers are reputable, however, and real bargains can be found if you know what you're looking for. New Yorkers shop at **J&R Music World** (23 Park Row, near City Hall), where you can find absolutely everything and the staff are knowledgeable; adjacent J&R stores sell cameras, computers, and anything else electronic you can imagine. Computer stores are concentrated on Fifth Avenue, above 20th Street. They include the **Apple Store** at 767 Fifth Avenue *(see page 41)*.

Department Stores. Macy's (34th and Broadway) and **Bloomingdale's** (59th and Lexington, and the new Soho location, at 504 Broadway) have everything; **Lord and**

Taylor (38th and Fifth Avenue) is a little smaller. **Barney's** (61st and Madison) is known for cutting-edge fashion and up-scale home furnishings. **Saks Fifth Avenue** (at 50th) is strictly high fashion for ladies who lunch and their gentlemen, as is **Bergdorf Goodman** (57th and Fifth Avenue). **Takashimaya** is a very chic Japanese alternative (Fifth Avenue near 54th).

Jewelry. Hit the Diamond District on West 47th for all prices and styles but not always bargains; Fifth Avenue above 50th Street is the location for the high-end jewelers (Cartier, Tiffany, Harry Winston, Bulgari, Van Cleef and Arpels). Small boutiques in Soho, Greenwich Village, and the East Village are good for hand-made originals.

Records and Books. With the advent of online retailing, the big record stores have shut down. The city does still have some small, independent music stores left with dedicated music lovers who keep them going like **Other Music** (15 East 4th Stret; tel 212-477-8150) and **Bleecker Street Records** (239 Bleecker Street at Carmine Street; tel: 212-255-7899).

In the book realm, **Barnes and Noble** has superstores catering to the masses (Union Square North, Sixth Avenue at 22nd Street, Broadway at 66th Street, Lexington at 86th Street,

Museum Shops

American Folk Art Museum, 45 West 53rd Street. Rural crafts and toys from around the country.

Metropolitan Museum of Art Gift Shop, in the museum on Fifth Avenue and also at Rockefeller Center (15 West 49th Street). Art books, posters, jewelry, reproductions.

The MoMA Design Store, 11 West 53rd Street and 44 West 53rd Street. Designer furniture and household articles *(see also page 40)*.

The Museum of the City of New York, Fifth Avenue at 103rd Street. The place to go to find old prints of the city.

and five more stores), as does **Borders** (Park Avenue and 57th Street, Columbus Circle in Time Warner Center, and three more stores). A new addition to the independent bookstore scene is the excellent **McNally Jackson** (52 Prince Street at Mulberry) in Nolita. Specialty bookstores all over the city cater to such tastes as theater (**Drama Book Shop** at 240 West 40th), mysteries (**Partners and Crime** on Greenwich Avenue), science fiction (**Forbidden Planet** on Broadway at 13th Street), and art (MoMA or any museum store). Young readers will love Books of Wonder (18th Street west of Fifth Avenue). For used books and out-of-print titles head for the renowned **Strand Book Store** (Broadway at 12th Street).

Jewelry heaven on Fifth Avenue

Toys. The ultimate toy store is **FAO Schwarz** (Fifth Avenue at 58th), where kids can design their own monsters and make their own dolls. They can also make their own music on the enormous 'Dance-On Piano'. The fun **Scholastic Store** in Soho features toys and books (557 Broadway).

Only in New York. The unassuming **Kiehl's** (Third Avenue between 13th and 14th) has the finest health and beauty products. **Zabar's** (Broadway between 80th and 81st) and **Dean & DeLuca** (560 Broadway in Soho) are fancy-food heavens. Broadway Panhandler (65 East 8th Street) has everything for your kitchen. Folks come from all over the world to shop at **Kate's Paperie** (72 Spring Street between Crosby and Lafayette and other locations in the city). Honestly, if **M&J Buttons** (Sixth Avenue between 37th and 38th) doesn't have the one you're looking for, it probably doesn't exist.

ENTERTAINMENT

They don't call New York the city that never sleeps for nothing. Whether you are interested in theater, the performing arts, a hot dance club, or just a quiet drink, you'll have plenty of opportunities to have fun once the sun goes down. There's no way to cover the entire New York nightlife scene in these few short paragraphs. But luckily, there are plenty of resources for finding out what's going on either before you arrive or once you've gotten to New York. The best places to find out what's going on during your stay are the Friday or Sunday *New York Times* (for mainstream events), *The New Yorker* or *New York* magazines (good for arts and more sophisticated clubs and bars), the *Village Voice* (an alternative weekly paper, especially strong on music), or *Time Out New York* (a weekly magazine with wide coverage of everything).

Tickets to most events can be purchased from Ticketmaster (tel: 800 745 3000 or www.ticketmaster.com), which charges a hefty service charge on top of the already hefty cost of the ticket itself. However, it is possible to purchase same-day tickets for Broadway and off-Broadway musicals and plays at substantial discounts *(see below)*.

Discount Theater Tickets

Discount theater tickets (up to 50 percent off) for same-day performances can be purchased at two TKTS locations in Manhattan. The most popular is in Duffy Square at 47th Street, which sells evening tickets after 3pm and matinee tickets after 10am daily. The other location is at South Street Seaport; it's open Mon–Sat 11am–6pm, Sun 11am–4pm (here they sell matinee tickets the day before the performance, and lines are usually shorter than in Times Square). They accept credit cards, cash, travelers checks or TKTS gift certificates.

Theater

The city that never sleeps

One of the most popular activities for visitors is to take in a **Broadway** or **off-Broadway** show. Broadway theaters are concentrated in the Times Square area, but smaller off-Broadway houses, where the offerings are increasingly interesting, are located all over town. Tickets for current hits must be booked ahead, sometimes months ahead. Curtain times are generally 8pm for evening performances, 2pm for matinees, which are usually on Wednesday, Saturday, and Sunday. Be prepared for sticker shock; the top shows charge over $100 for their best seats, and American theaters often do not follow the lead of the world by charging less for the less desirable seats.

Classical Music and Dance

New York has a particularly vibrant and diverse music scene, offering every kind of style imaginable, from opera and classical music to jazz, pop, blues, country, world, and reggae. Admission to many of the concerts is free: the summer concerts in Central Park, for instance, or the lunch-time concerts held in the Financial District and midtown, which liven up the day for office workers.

New York City's two major opera companies are the **Metropolitan Opera** and the **New York City Opera**. They occupy adjacent buildings at Lincoln Center. If you want to see world-famous artists, go to the Met, but the City Opera also has done some fine work of late. As for classical music concerts, you're likely to find a dozen or so scheduled for a single evening – often at **Carnegie Hall** (57th Street and Seventh Avenue).

You'll have more chances to see good dance performances in New York than in almost any other city in the world, from the **American Ballet Theater** and **New York City Ballet** (both at Lincoln Center) to modern dance companies, many of which present their seasons at the **Joyce Theater** on Eighth Avenue (at 19th Street) and at **City Center** on Seventh Avenue (at 55th Street). And one should not forget such notable companies as those of Alvin Ailey, the Dance Theater of Harlem, Merce Cunningham, Mark Morris, and Paul Taylor.

Taxis in Times Square

Film

There are hundreds of mainstream movie screens in New York, but here you'll also have the chance to see many films that might not make it to your local multiplex. **MoMA**, the **Walter Reade Theater** at Lincoln Center, and the **Museum of the Moving Image** in Queens all have ongoing film series, mostly revivals of classic and art films. Other places to find movies that you might not otherwise see are: **Film Forum** (209 West Houston, between Sixth Avenue and Varick, tel: 212-727-8110); **Lincoln Plaza** (Broadway between 62nd and 63rd, tel: 212-757-2280); the **Quad Cinema** (34 West 13th Street, between Fifth and Sixth avenues, tel: 212-255-8800); and the **Angelika Film Center** (Houston and Mercer streets, tel: 212-995-2000). And there are others.

Dance Clubs

The thing to keep in mind about dance clubs in New York is that clubs can be quite different depending on when and where you go. Among the hundreds of ever-changing venues (and themes), you might consider trendy (**Marquee**, 289 Tenth Avenue between 26th and 27th), house (**Cielo**, 18 Little West 12th Street), or mainstream (**China Club** at 268 West 47th Street). And, there is always the megaclub **Home** (532 West 27th Street between Tenth and Eleventh avenues).

Cabarets and Jazz Clubs

New York is perhaps *the* center of world jazz. Listen to Jazz at **Iridium** (1650 Broadway at 51st Street), the **Village Vanguard** (178 Seventh Avenue South), the Blue Note (131 West 3rd Street), or **Birdland** (314 West 44th Street). Some other places where you can hear good music while you drink and/or dine include the **Oak Room** (59 West 44th Street in the Algonquin Hotel), **Joe's Pub** (in the Public Theater, Lafayette Street at Astor Place), or **Café Carlyle** (35 East 76th Street).

Bars

Hotel bars have made a comeback in New York, and they are now some of the hottest places to go. Most are pretty swank, so bring your gold card. New bars have opened at the Shoreham, Mansfield, and W – The Court hotels. The lobby bars at the Royalton and Four Seasons hotels are fashionable places to meet. Monkey Bar at the Hotel Elysée (60 East 54th Street) and the Paramount Bar in the Paramount Hotel (235 West 46th Street) are old standbys.

Venture to the **East Village**, and you'll find a good variety of bars: old-fashioned (McSorley's Old Ale House at 15 East 7th Street), relaxed (Von, 3 Bleeker Street), underground (Pravda at 281 Lafayette Street), and fun (Otto's Shrunken Head, 538 East 14th Street). **Greenwich Village** and the **West Village** offer a full range, from the brewpub (Heartland Brewery, 35 Union Square West) to the cozy beer-lovers' bar (Blind Tiger Ale House, 281 Bleecker Street at Jones Street) to the speakeasy-esque (Employees Only, 510 Hudson Street). **Chelsea** offers the whole gamut from gay with dancing (Splash at 50 West 17th Street) to gay without attitude (Barracuda at 275 West 22nd Street). And then there are bars for everyone, such as the Brass

Serving Cocktails at the Brass Monkey Bar

Monkey Bar in the **Meatpacking District** (55 Little West 12th Street), a relaxing place to enjoy a beer and a burger.

Tried-and-true choices for impromptu celebrations with friends include the Bubble Lounge (228 West Broadway) for champagne, and the Lenox Lounge (288 Lenox Avenue) for uptown ambiance with jazz.

SPORTS

Watching Sports

Baseball season is from April through September, and NYC has two major-league teams. The **Mets** play at Citi Field Stadium in Queens (take the 7 subway right to the stadium), and the **Yankees** play in the Bronx (the 4 and D subway lines stop at the stadium). You can usually buy tickets at the stadium on game day.

Football season runs from September through January. New York City has no professional football teams, but two play nearby in New Jersey's Meadowlands. The **Jets** and the **Giants** both play in Giants Stadium (there's a shuttle-bus service from the Port Authority). Basketball season runs from October through April, and the **New York Knicks** play at Madison Square Garden at 33rd Street and Seventh Avenue. Tickets are hard to come by, but you can try the box office. Hockey season generally runs from October to April; the New York team is the **Rangers**, and they play at Madison Square Garden as well. The **US Open Tennis championships** are played at the US Tennis Center in Queens (7 subway to Mets-Willets Point) in early September.

Playing Sports

Chances are, you didn't come to New York for the great outdoors, but when New Yorkers want to be active they go to **Central Park**, where you can hire a bicycle or a boat (both

All aboard for the Statue of Liberty

near the Loeb Boathouse, mid-Park near the Bethesda Terrace), or, in the winter, ice skates (at **Wollman Rink**, mid-Park at 63rd, or **Lasker Rink**, 110th and Lenox Avenue). Otherwise, you can just follow the example of the thousands of New Yorkers who jog, bike, and skate in Central Park and along the city pavements. **Bowlmor Lanes** at 110 University Place in Greenwich Village has 44 bowling lanes and tennis courts upstairs.

Chelsea Piers (23rd Street at the Hudson River) is the one all-purpose destination for all your sporting needs. You'll find facilities for virtually every sport imaginable, including skating, horseback riding, and swimming. For a complete run-down, tel: 212-336-6666.

New York from the Water

For children and adults alike, seeing Manhattan from the water is an experience not to be missed. There are great views from the Statue of Liberty and Staten Island ferries *(see page 28)*. In addition, **Circle Line Cruises** (tel: 212-563-3200; www.circleline42.com) offers various options, including 3-hour Full Island Cruise (right around Manhattan), the 2-hour Semi-Circle Cruise, and the sunset Harbour Lights Cruise. Cruises leave from Pier 83 at 42nd Street and Twelfth Avenue. **NY Waterway** (tel: 800-533 3779; www.nywaterway.com) runs regular tours from Pier 78 at 38th Street and Twelfth Avenue, including a Friday night dance party cruise.

CHILDREN'S NEW YORK

New York City parks are a great escape for kids. **Central Park** offers the greatest number of attractions including the Central Park Zoo and the Carousel. Young visitors will not want to miss climbing the larger-than-life sculpture of Alice in Wonderland. **Nelson A. Rockefeller Park** in Battery Park City (Chambers Street and Hudson River) has a great children's playground and lots of open space to run and play. **Madison Square Park** (25th and Madison Avenue) and **Hudson River Park Playground** (Pier 51, Gansevoort Street and Hudson River) are favourites of New York City kids.

Almost all of New York's museums have exciting offerings for kids. There are also museums devoted entirely to children. The **Children's Museum of Manhattan** (Tue–Sun 10am–5pm; charge; cmom.org) is large and very popular. Kids can design their own subway mosaic art, build their own amusement park while learning about physics or climb a giant Trojan horse while learning about ancient Greece. The **Brooklyn Children's Museum** (Tue–Fri 11am–5pm, Sat–Sun 10am–5pm); charge; www.brooklynkids.org) is the oldest museum created expressly for kids. It underwent a major expansion and renovation in 2008, and kids will love the interactive exhibits like World Brooklyn, a cityscape with kid-sized stores.

For children's theatre try the **New Victory Theater** (www.newvictory.org), which makes an effort to present exciting and engaging performances. The **Manhattan Children's Theatre** (www.mctny.org) offers a selection of both classics and new works during their September-May season.

Many bookstores including the large chains have children's story hours. Young readers will enjoy exploring the sprawling **Scholastic Store** (557 Broadway) in Soho. **Books of Wonder** (18 West 18th Street) is the city's oldest and largest independent children's bookstore.

Calendar of Events

January Chinese New Year parades and celebrations (Chinatown, Mott, Mulberry and Bayard Streets), late January to mid-February.
March St Patrick's Day Parade (Fifth Avenue) on March 17. Whitney Biennial (in even years, 2010, 2012), Whitney Museum of American Art).
April Cherry Blossom Festival (Sakura Matsuri; Brooklyn Botanic Garden), mid–late April. Tribeca Film Festival (various locations), late Apr–early May.
May Ninth Avenue International Food Festival (9th Avenue/37th to 57th streets), early to mid-May. Fleet Week, late May.
June Gay and Lesbian Pride Day Parade (Fifth Avenue & West Village), usually last Sunday in June. Museum Mile Festival (Fifth Avenue/82nd and 105th Streets), usually 2nd Tuesday in June. SummerStage (Central Park), June through August. Shakespeare in the Park (The Delacorte Theater in Central Park), June through August.
July Macy's Fourth of July Fireworks (Hudson River), July 4th. Lincoln Center Festival (Lincoln Center), throughout July. Midsummer Night's Swing (Lincoln Center), throughout July. Mostly Mozart Festival (Lincoln Center), late July- August.
August Harlem Week and Harlem Jazz and Music Festival (venues throughout Harlem), throughout August. New York International Fringe Festival (various downtown venues), late August. US Open Tennis Championship (Flushing Meadows, Queens), late August–early September
September Feast of San Gennaro (Little Italy), late September. New York Film Festival (Lincoln Center venues), late September to early October.
October Halloween Parade (Greenwich Village, Sixth Avenue/Spring and 23rd Streets), October 31.
November New York City Marathon (throughout city), 1st Sunday in November. Macy's Thanksgiving Day Parade (77th Street and Central Park to Broadway and 34th Street), Thanksgiving Day. Radio City Music Hall Christmas Spectacular (Radio City Music Hall), throughout November and December.
December Christmas Tree Lighting (Rockefeller Center), late November/early December. New Year's Eve (Times Square), December 31.

EATING OUT

In a city with more than 20,000 restaurants, New Yorkers dine out a lot. With restaurants just steps from their doors there is no reason for them not to enjoy the best the city has to offer, and visitors should do the same. You'll find some of the best restaurants in the country in New York, and some are quite expensive. But you won't have to take out a second mortgage on your home to eat well in this city – even in Manhattan. The variety of restaurants and eating options is unsurpassed. You can enjoy Indian dosas from a street vendor, dine at the newest celebrity chef's restaurant, or simply enjoy a really great meal at a favorite neighborhood spot.

Price

You can eat very well in New York for a modest amount of money. The average price of dinner (including one drink and tip) is around $40. A good way to experience some of the best (and often most expensive) restaurants without blowing your budget is to drop in for lunch instead of dinner. The lunch menu is almost always cheaper. For example, a 3-course lunch at Oceana costs $48; for dinner the price tag goes up to $78, even though the quality and variety of the offerings are very similar. Prix fixe meals, particularly pre-theater dinners (usually served 6–7pm) are vastly

A New York diner

Restaurant guide

The Zagat Survey of New York City Restaurants is one of the best in the Zagat series of reference guides. Published annually, the book solicits from local restaurant-goers (in New York this is a large, avid, and opinionated group) to produce a compendium that is fairly comprehensive and quite informative. The basic information from the guide (excluding reviews, unless you are a registered member) is available online at: www.zagat.com.

cheaper than the à la carte menu and are being offered with increasing frequency. If food is the focus of your trip, then plan your visit around one of the seasonal 'NYC Restaurant Weeks,' when more than 200 top-end restaurants offer bargain three-course prix fixe lunches (around $25) and dinners (around $35). If you are watching your budget, then always choose tap water when offered the choice between bottled water or tap. It is a perfectly safe option.

Meals and Meal Times

Breakfast is usually served from 7am through at least 9am. Brunch is usually just on weekends, 11am–3pm. Lunch is generally noon–2pm. Dinner is served anywhere from 5.30pm until 11pm, or later in some places. New Yorkers tend to eat dinner a bit later than elsewhere in the US and you'll find restaurants busiest between 7pm and 9pm.

NEW YORK SPECIALTIES

Iconic Delis & the Pastrami Sandwich

Pastrami with mustard on rye: the quintessential New York sandwich. Delis all over the United States lay claim to a New York-style pastrami sandwich. But, of course, the best are served in authentic New York delicatessens where you will pay around $15 for a sandwich. Pastrami starts first with corned beef (beef brisket soaked in brine), which is then smoked to give it its unique flavor. It is sliced thick or thin (usually your choice) and served with mustard on rye for a tender and juicy melt-in-your-mouth sandwich. The Eastern European tradition of salted and cured meats was brought to New York by early immigrants. Katz's deli in the lower East Side opened in 1888 and was immortalized in the famous deli scene in the film *When Harry Met Sally*. While the heyday of the New York deli – when struggling actors rubbed shoulders with celebrities, presidents, and New York movers and shakers – may have passed, it's not too late to visit one of these iconic delis: **The Stage** (834 Seventh Avenue between 53rd and 54th streets, tel: 212-245-7850); **The Carnegie** (854 Seventh Avenue at 55th Street, tel: 800-234-5606); **Katz's** (205 East Houston at Ludlow, tel: 212-254-2246).

The pastrami sandwich – a New York institution

Diners and Coffee Shops

You'll find them dotted all over New York, with vast menus and reasonable prices, in every neighborhood. The diner immortalized in the comedy *Seinfeld* is **Tom's Restaurant** (2880 Broadway at 112th Street).

Bakeries

You'll find lovely bakeries in lots of city neighborhoods. They are great places to pick up a sandwich, breakfast pastry, or sweet cupcake treat. **Once Upon a Tart** (135 Sullivan Street), in Soho, offers tarts, sandwiches, scones, and other treats, which you can grab to go, or eat at one of the outdoor tables while watching the Soho scene. **Le Pain Quotidien** (14 locations in Manhattan) is a Belgian chain where you'll sit at communal tables and enjoy delicious fresh bread, tarts, and pastries.

Bagels

Bagels were allegedly invented in New York, and the best examples can still be found here; aficionados argue about where the perfect bagel can be found, but you won't go wrong with **Ess-a-Bagel** (359 First Avenue or 831 Third Avenue), **H&H** (2239 Broadway), or one of the many neigh-

Brunch

If you are in New York over a weekend, then you should try to have Saturday or Sunday brunch. New Yorkers love lazy weekend brunches, which are served at most restaurants usually starting at 11am (sometimes earlier) through late afternoon (3–4pm). Take the hefty Sunday *New York Times* with you and enjoy. Best to try to go earlier than noon if you don't want to wait. It's normal to see groups of people waiting patiently outside their favorite brunch spots. Diners also offer good brunch options.

borhood bagel shops. All that can be said for certain is that bagels need to be fresh (no more than a day old), so stick to the shops that make their own. Add cream cheese and lox (smoked salmon) and you have a great New York meal.

Bagels and more at a bakery

Pizza

New York is known for pizza, though as anyone who's ever bought a tepid slice from one of the city's pizzerias can tell you, it's not all of the best quality. But there *is* infinite variety, from thin crust to thick and chewy to artisanal, oven-baked pizzas. **John's** (278 Bleecker Street) will never do you wrong, though you'll have to buy a whole pie – they don't sell single slices. In Little Italy, **Lombardi's** (32 Spring Street) expanded space means more diners can enjoy their popular clam pie. **Grimaldi's** (19 Old Fulton Street) in Brooklyn, at the foot of the Brooklyn Bridge, is a perfect treat after a walk over the bridge.

New York Cheesecake

This is the classic, New York comfort food, available almost everywhere in many variations. A graham cracker crumb crust is topped with a rich, smooth cheesecake to make a delicious treat. **Junior's** (Times Square, West 46th Street between Broadway and Eighth Avenue, or the original location in Brooklyn, 386 Flatbush Street at Dekalb Avenue) shouldn't be missed.

Steakhouses

Carnivores will delight in the almost 100 steakhouse options in New York. One of the best in the current artisanal-beef trend is **Craftsteak** (85 Tenth Avenue at 15th Street). **Old Homestead** (56 Ninth Avenue) is a classic, as is **Peter Luger** (178 Broadway at Driggs Street) in Williamsburg, Brooklyn, which continues its reign as New York's best.

Burgers and Dawgs

The perfect budget meal, the hot dog makes you feel like a real New Yorker, whether you are grabbing one at Yankee Stadium or making a pit stop at Gray's Papaya after a night of dancing. The following are all good options: the quirky **Dawgs on Park** (178 East 7th Street in the East Village) with its wide range of specialty dogs; the venerable **Papaya King** (corner of Seventh Avenue and 14th Street, 179 East 86th Street, 121 West 125th Street); and the excellent value **Gray's Papaya** (2090 Broadway and 402 Sixth Avenue).

Dawgs in the East Village

Burger joints seem to be opening all the time. You'll find burgers served in restaurants in every price range, from the very top restaurants to the seasonal Shake Shack in Madison Square Park. The following all serve highly rated burgers: the burger joint at **Le Parker**

Meridien (119 West 56th Street between Sixth and Seventh avenues); **Rare Bar & Grill** (in Shelburne Murray Hill Hotel, 303 Lexington Avenue at 37th Street; 228 Bleecker Street between Carmine Street and Sixth Avenue); **BLT Burger** (470 Sixth Avenue between 11th and 12th streets); and the **Shake Shack** (open April–October) food stand in Madison Square Park (southeast corner on Madison Avenue and 23rd Street).

The quintessential New York cheap eat: the burger

Carts

Some of the best food in New York is served on sidewalks – and it's not just hot dogs and pretzels. You can find Indian dosas, bratwurst, kebabs, steamed rolled rice noodles, and Mexican tamales. Many of the best vendors are located in the outer boroughs (Queens, in particular) but there are a fair share in Manhattan. Just look for the cart with the line and follow the New Yorkers. Many New Yorkers pick up their breakfast on the street from carts serving coffee, bagels, muffins, and breakfast pastries. A small coffee costs less than $1, which is about as cheap as you'll get.

Healthy Fast Food Options

The following are all reliable, quick, relatively healthy, and inexpensive options while on the go: **Au Bon Pain** is a bakery/café chain serving quality soups, salads, rice and pasta dishes, sandwiches, and pastries at many locations throughout the city; **Hale and Hearty Soups** (several locations in midtown) serves above-average soup that is well worth the price; and **Whole Foods Market** (Union Square on 14th Street; 95 East Houston Street at Bowery; 250 Seventh Avenue; Columbus Circle downstairs) is a chain of natural foods supermarket in brilliant locations with convenient self-serve cafeterias.

ETHNIC ENCLAVES

Chinatown *(see page 69)* is the best-known locale for Chinese cuisine in New York, but less well publicized is Flushing, Queens, where a number of very good Chinese restaurants are located. You'll find a group of Vietnamese restaurants on Baxter Street, Chinatown, not far from the US Courthouse.

Though **Little Italy** has shrunk to a couple of blocks of Mulberry Street north of Canal Street, there are still Italian restaurants that can pass muster; most of the places here will do if all you want is a plate of pasta and a glass of wine. Another group of Italian restaurants can be found on Bleecker Street between Thompson Street and Seventh Avenue.

Little India, on Sixth Street between First and Second avenues, has a selection of very cheap Indian restaurants, only a handful of which are actually good (Panna II at 93 First Avenue, the one with a million chili-pepper lights, is one of the best); another place to look for Indian restaurants is Lexington Avenue in the 20s (Madras Mahal at 104 Lexington Avenue, though inconsistent, has reliably good dosas).

The above are just the most obvious cuisines, but food from all over the world is available somewhere in New York. For example, Brazilian restaurants can be found in a group on 45th and 46th streets in Midtown (between Sixth and Seventh avenues), while Egyptian fare is concentrated over in Long Island City. For a reasonably priced multi-ethnic feast, investigate Ninth Avenue in the 40s and 50s.

PLACES TO EAT

We have used the following symbols to give an idea of the average price for a three-course meal for one, not including drinks or tip:

$$$$ 50–100 dollars	$$ 25–35 dollars
$$$ 35–50 dollars	$ below 25 dollars

MIDTOWN

Adour at the St Regis $$$$ *2 East 55th Street (at 5th Avenue), tel: 212-710-2277, www.adour-stregis.com.* A match made in cuisine heaven: the five-star St Regis hotel marries the five-star French chef Alain Ducasse at prices to match.

Becco $$–$$$ *355 West 46th Street (8th and 9th avenues), tel: 212-397-7597; www.becco-nyc.com.* Come for the delicious pasta at this rustic Theater District favorite that combines reasonable prices and high quality. The two-course fixed-price meal is particularly good value, especially since the pasta is an all-you-can-eat special.

Carmine's $$$ *200 West 44th Street (Broadway and 8th Avenue), tel: 212-221-3800; www.carminesnyc.com.* The huge portions of hearty Italian food at this Theater District favorite are served family-style, so the prices aren't as high as they seem at first glance. Always mobbed and loud, but consistently churning out massive quantities of food at all hours, this is a reliable standby eaterie. Be warned, however: The no-reservations policy can lead to long waits.

Churrascaria Plataforma $$$$ *316 West 49th Street (8th and 9th avenues), tel: 212-245-0505; www.churrascariaplataforma.com.* All-you-can eat Brazilian *rodízios* (huge meat-heavy buffet) make this one of the most popular and fun places to go when you are in the mood to eat, and eat a lot. Start at the salad bar, but then turn your dish over to begin the parade of skewered meats, and don't stop until you're about to explode. A *caipirinha* cocktail will set your taste buds on the right track.

DB Bistro Moderne $$$$ *55 West 44th Street (between 5th and 6th avenues), tel: 212-391-2400; www.danielnyc.com/dbbistro.* So moderne that the menu is organized by ingredients. Chef Daniel Boulud's bistro is awash in culinary surprises and Art Deco glitz, with a clientele to match.

Four Seasons $$$$ *99 East 52nd St (between Lexington and Park avenues), tel: 212-754-9494; www.fourseasonsrestaurant.com.* Since it opened nearly 50 years ago, the Four Seasons in the landmark Seagram Building has had a clientele that rivals any Who's Who listing. The decor is priceless and Chef Christian Albin's American seasonal specialties served in the elegant pool room or the grill room are impeccable.

Fred's at Barney's $$$ *660 Madison Avenue, 9th floor (at 60th in Barney's), tel: 212-833-2200; www.barneys.com.* This lunch spot in Barney's department store is wildly popular, and justifiably so. The antipasto plate is a real charmer, but the Madison Avenue chopped salad with Italian tuna and the more substantial options are also very good. Don't miss dessert. Dinner is also served, but only until 9pm.

Jewel of India $–$$$ *15 West 44th Street (between 5th and 6th avenues), tel: 212-869-5544; www.jewelofindiarestaurant.com.* A quiet and elegant Indian restaurant, the Jewel of India can be quite expensive when you order from the à-la-carte menu, but both the lunch buffet and the pre-theater fixed-price dinner (5.30–7pm) allow you to enjoy the fine cuisine at more down-to-earth prices.

Le Bernardin $$$$ *155 West 51st Street, tel: 212-554-1515; www.le-bernardin.com.* Arguably one of the finest restaurants in the city, Le Bernardin serves only seafood. Every item on the fixed-price menu is a winner, from the simplest pan-seared cod to a whole-roasted red snapper for two. Divinely inspired desserts. No lunch Sat–Sun. Closed Sun.

Smith and Wollensky $$$$ *797 3rd Avenue (at 49th), tel: 212-753-1530; www.smithandwollensky.com.* The well-aged steaks served in this male-dominated classic eaterie are consistently and perfectly grilled. The wine list is also excellent, although expensive – sometimes shockingly so. The less expensive grill just around the corner on 49th Street is a good alternative for anyone without an expense account.

Virgil's Real BBQ $$–$$$ *152 West 44th Street (near Broadway), tel: 212-921-9494; www.virgilsbbq.com.* Something to appeal to nearly all carnivores. The dry-smoked ribs and brisket are good, but the pulled pork is a favorite. Share the 'pig out' platter to get a taste of everything, and have cobbler for dessert.

Zen Palate $$ *663 9th Avenue (at 46th Street), tel: 212-582-1669; www.zenpalate.com.* An Asian-based vegetarian restaurant started by a group of Buddhist vegetarians. It offers a good range of healthy menu options. There is another location downtown near South Street Seaport at 104 John Street (at Cliff Street, tel: 212-962-4208).

DOWNTOWN

Blue Water Grill $$$–$$$$ *31 Union Square West (at 16th), tel: 212-675-9500; www.brguestrestaurants.com.* Housed in a spacious former bank, this popular Union Square seafood restaurant is consistently crowded. The raw offerings are especially good. The prices are on the high side of moderate but still quite reasonable. Reservations are necessary unless you want to sit outside.

Cafeteria $$ *119 7th Avenue (at 17th), tel: 212-414-1717, www.cafeteriagroup.com.* One of Chelsea's trendy options, Cafeteria is open 24 hours and offers reconstructed bistro and diner food for hip club-goers (where else will you be able to get pancakes or grilled salmon at 4.30am?) Consistently good, if not overly exciting.

Chanterelle $$$$ *2 Harrison Street (at Hudson Street), tel: 212-966-6960; www.chanterellenyc.com.* Thirty years ago, this was Tribeca's first serious, luxury French restaurant, and it has never dropped its standards. Worth every expensive dollar, but there's a deal to be had at a prix-fixe lunch.

Counter $$–$$$ *105 1st Avenue (between 6th and 7th), tel: 212-982-5870; www.counternyc.com*. Mellow and relaxed, this East Village vegetarian serves fare ranging from healthy comfort to innovative. Even meat eaters will be satisfied with the flavorful dishes. Also features organic wines.

Cucina di Pesce $–$$ *87 East 4th Street (near 2nd Avenue), tel: 212-260-6800; www.cucinadipesce.com*. This busy East Village Italian favorite is nothing fancy, but with virtually every main course under $10, what else could you ask for? Pastas and fish are all good. Free mussels for those waiting at the bar. Cash only.

Do Hwa $$–$$$ *55 Carmine Street (between Bedford Street and 7th Avenue), tel: 212 414 1224; www.dohwanyc.com*. Excellent home-cooking Korean-style ensures that this restaurant, with minimalist design, is always busy. Tasting menus offer a good introduction. Or ask for a table with a built-in grill. The classic *bibimbop* served in a hot stone dish is a favourite.

East of Eighth $$ *254 West 23rd Street (near 8th Avenue), tel: 212-352-0075*. One of the most consistently good (and crowded) restaurants in Chelsea, East of Eighth offers pasta, pizza, and other Italian-inspired fare at moderate prices. The pre-theater menu is a real bargain, especially when you purchase discount movie tickets for the Clearview cinema next door.

Gotham Bar and Grill $$$$ *12 East 12th Street (5th Avenue and University), tel: 212-620-4020; www.gothambarandgrill.com*. This large, airy space is usually filled with well-dressed downtowners who appreciate the exquisite (and very tall) food and well-chosen but expensive wines. Few other upscale restaurants are as inviting to single diners, who can order and eat at the bar in comfort and style. The $25 fixed-price restaurant week lunch is a great deal.

Gramercy Tavern $$$$ *42 E. 20th Street (between Broadway & Park). tel: 212 477 0777; www.gramercytavern.com*. Seasonally inspired fresh and local ingredients are the focus of this popular New American tavern with excellent service. Reservations are often difficult to come by but you can also eat in the front tavern which accepts walk-in basis. Offers prix fixe menus for lunch and dinner as well as tasting menus.

Hangawi $$$ *12 East 32nd Street (5th and Madison avenues), tel: 212-213-0077; www.hangawirestaurant.com.* Diners at this vegetarian Korean restaurant will quickly become suffused with a Zen-like calm. Discard your cares (and your shoes) at the door, and try mountain-root vegetables, porridges, and other delicacies.

Kanoyama $$$$ *175 2nd Avenue (at 11th), tel: 212-777-5266; www.kanoyama.com.* East Village Japanese restaurant that is rapidly becoming a local favorite. The portions are generous and fish is incredibly fresh. Friendly staff.

L'Ecole $$–$$$ *462 Broadway (at Grand), tel: 212-219-3300; www.frenchculinary.com.* L'Ecole is a firm favorite thanks to its moderate prices, carefully composed wine list (among the most reasonable in town), and consistently good French food. Operated as a training center for the French Culinary Institute, its shaky service can be easily forgiven when the check arrives. Where else can you get five (yes, five) courses for just $42?

Nobu $$$$ *105 Hudson Street (at Franklin), tel: 212-219-0500; www.noburestaurants.com.* Still wildly popular and trendy (forget Saturday night), Nobu continues to pack in crowds with its innovative nouvelle Japanese menu. Next Door Nobu offers a slightly less expensive menu and a no-reservations policy (for those who won't be dining with Robert De Niro), as long as you don't mind standing in line.

Noodle Village $ *13 Mott Street (near Chatham Square) tel: 212-233-0788; www.noodlevillagenyc.com.* This new Cantonese restaurant at the southern end of Mott Street in Chinatown boasts that their chef arrived straight from Hong Kong. They also proudly claim that there is no MSG added to their dishes. The congee and noodle soups are popular choices. A great cheap, healthy and fast option.

Nyonya $ *194 Grand Street (at Mulberry), tel: 212-334-3669, www.penangusa.com.* The place to go for an introduction to the delicious (and sometimes spicy) cuisine of Malaysia. The Hainanese chicken is good, but don't overlook spicy beef *rendang* or one of the equally tasty seafood dishes.

Red $$ *19 Fulton Street (at Front), tel: 212-571-5900; www.ark restaurants.com.* In the culinary wasteland of the South Street Seaport, this southwestern spot is at least attractive and fun. The food is reasonably good and not as overpriced as most of the other choices in the area, so grab a margarita and relax.

Shabu-Tatsu $$ *216 East 10th Street (between 1st and 2nd avenues), tel: 212-477-2972.* At this small, popular Japanese restaurant, diners choose a selection of thinly sliced meats and vegetables for *shabu-shabu* (swirled in a hot pot of seasoned water), *sukiyaki* (a Japanese stew), or *yakiniku* (cooked on a grill) and cook it themselves in the middle of the table.

Shanghai Cuisine $ *89 Bayard Street (at Mulberry), tel: 212-732-8988.* Shanghai cuisine is more than just soup and dumplings, as this Chinatown spot proves. Fresh interpretations of traditional specialties, including smoked fish and mock duck, will reward the adventurous. Cash only.

Spice Market $$$$ *403 West 13th Street (at 9th Avenue), tel: 212-675-2322; www.spicemarketnewyork.com.* A Meatpacking District destination from Jean-Georges Vongerichten celebrating Thai-Malay street food in a sumptuous and opulent setting with prices to match. Difficult to get reservations – you need to book well in advance if you are hoping to eat here during your New York visit.

Union Square Café $$$$ *21 East 16th Street (near Union Square), tel: 212-243-4020; www.unionsquarecafe.com.* Gracious service and reliably good food are two reasons this is one of New York's perennially favorite restaurants. Although the Mediterranean-inspired cuisine is no longer cutting-edge, the food still dazzles in unexpected ways. Even the fried calamari, now a restaurant staple, is heads above the chewy appetizer most people have come to expect. The extensive and reasonably priced wine list is an added bonus.

THE UPPER EAST SIDE

Boathouse $$$–$$$$ *Central Park, enter on East 72nd Street, tel: 212-517-2233; www.thecentralparkboathouse.com.* The lake and surrounding greenery of Central Park are the most memorable part of a meal in this airy, glass-fronted dining room and waterside terrace (the perfect spot for a warm-weather brunch). True to the watery surroundings, the kitchen sends out such nautically inspired flourishes as sea urchin and caviar in a scallop shell and pan-roasted monkfish and seared wild striped sea bass. Meanwhile, brunchtime hits of the French toast and omelet variety satisfy the hungry weekend crowds.

Café Boulud $$$$ *20 East 76th Street (near Madison Avenue, in the Surrey Hotel), tel: 212-772-2600; www.danielnyc.com.* Daniel Boulud has also mastered the art of casual elegance. Calling this a tarted-up bistro (which is what it is) strikes a note of sacrilege, but the label can't detract from what a great chef can produce when he takes his gloves off.

Café Sabarsky $$$ *1048 5th Avenue (at 86th Street), tel: 212-288-0665; www.wallserestaurant.com.* Enter this wood-paneled salon within the Neue Gallerie *(see page 54)*, and you'll think you're on Vienna's Ringstrasse. Chef Kurt Gutenbrunner lives up to the surroundings, and the beef goulash, Viennese sausage, linzer torte, and other fare from the banks of the Danube take museum food to new heights.

Candle Café $$ *1307 3rd Avenue (between 74th and 75th streets), tel: 212-472-0970; www.candlecafe.com.* The staff at this small bastion of health serve up innovative, tasty vegan fare. Even carnivores might be tempted by the stir-fried tempeh with peanut sauce and casseroles of sweet potatoes and steamed greens, not to mention the desserts.

Sarabeth's $$–$$$ *1295 Madison Avenue (at East 92nd Street), tel: 212-410-7335; www.sarabeths.com.* Cheery and incredibly popular, Sarabeth's is best for its home-style breakfasts and brunch, from waffles to fluffy eggs, although succulent roasts and other serious and well-prepared dishes come out at dinner time. Child-friendly environs and homey decor. There are two other locations: at 423 Amsterdam Avenue, between 80th and 81st streets, tel: 212-496-6280, and in the Whitney Museum at 945 Madison Avenue at 75th Street, tel: 212-570-3670. There is also Sarabeth's Bakery, at Chelsea Market, 75 9th Avenue (between 15th and 16th streets), tel: 212-989-2424.

Sfoglia $$$$ *1402 Lexington Avenue (at 92nd Street), tel: 212-831-1402; www.sfogliarestaurant.com.* This New York branch of the owners' Nantucket restaurant has quickly become a neighborhood favorite. This unobtrusive little trattoria offering seasonal Northern Italian country fare in a down-home, casual and intimate setting brings diners back again and again to sample the inventive menu, which changes regularly. There are only ten tables so plan ahead for dinner reservations. The homemade bread is to die for.

THE UPPER WEST SIDE

Dovetail $$$–$$$$ *103 West 77th Street (at Columbus Ave), tel: 212-362-3800, www.dovetailnyc.com.* A very welcome addition to the Upper West Side just a block from the American Museum of Natural History. John Fraser's skilled execution using farm-fresh ingredients served in an intimate setting has garnered critical acclaim. Gordon Ramsay chose him as an emerging chef to watch. The 3-course Sunday Suppa for $38 is superb value. But you can't go wrong on other nights with the 5-course $88 tasting menu.

Barney Greengrass $$ *541 Amsterdam Avenue (between 86th and 87th streets), tel: 212-724-4707, www.barneygreengrass.com.* The faded murals and formica tables are deceptively downbeat, but New Yorkers continue to herald this West Side institution as the best place in town for lox, smoked sturgeon, chopped liver, and other Jewish fare. Weekend lines are long, but in them you might spot Bill Murray, Woody Allen, and other celebrity regulars. Closed Monday.

Jean-Georges $$$$ *1 Central Park West (at 60th and 61st streets, in the Trump Interantional Hotel), tel: 212-299-3900, www.jean-georges.com.* Chef Jean-Georges Vongerichten's four-star experiment in ultra-chic surroundings is well worth the price. For the ultimate, try the seven-course tasting menu; for the experience of just being here, order the prix-fixe lunch at a fraction of the cost.

Lemongrass Grill $ *2534 Broadway (between 94th and 95th streets), tel: 212-666-0888.* This reasonably priced Thai chain can be found all over the city. Good bets include lemongrass pork chops (diners share them), spring rolls, and pad Thai. Other locations of the Lemongrass Grill are on 34th Street (between 3rd and Lexington avenues), 9 East 13th Street (between 5th Avenue and University Place), and 84 William Street (at Maiden Lane).

Shun Lee West $$$$ *43 West 65th Street (Columbus Avenue and Central Park West), tel: 212-595-8895; www.shunleewest.com.* Those used to take-out noodles, fried rice, and General Tso's chicken will be amazed at how refined Chinese food can be. Attached to the original restaurant is the much less expensive Shun Lee Café, and on the east side is Shun Lee Palace (155 East 55th Street between Lexington and 3rd avenues, tel: 212-371-8844).

Tavern on the Green $$$–$$$$ *Central Park at West 67th Street, tel: 212-873-3200; www.tavernonthegreen.com.* Even native New Yorkers feel like tourists out for a big night at this Central Park lair, bedecked with fairy lights. The fact that the Tavern's steak and fish fare is run-of-the-mill is more than compensated for by the festive atmosphere and setting, which is all the more magical if you get a table on the summertime terrace. Reservations recommended.

A–Z TRAVEL TIPS

A Summary of Practical Information

A

ACCOMMODATIONS *(See also* YOUTH HOSTELS AND YMCAS *and the list of* RECOMMENDED HOTELS *starting on page 125)*

A decent yet reasonably priced hotel room in New York is increasingly difficult to find. The average price of a hotel room in Manhattan is now just over $300 per night. The high season is fall and winter, particularly from late November through New Year's Day, when rates can be as much as 25 percent higher; the low season is January through mid-March, though some hotels also reduce rates in the summer. Advance reservations are often crucial; the city is very crowded at all times. Be aware that quoted rates will not include a sales tax of 14.25 percent, plus a $3.50 per day occupancy tax. Most hotels do not provide breakfast, but there are a few exceptions. At many hotels children can sleep in their parents' room at no extra charge.

You can also find bed and breakfasts in the city. However their rates ($150–$300) can vary quite dramatically and can, in some cases, be higher than many hotel rates. It's a good option if you want to feel part of the city and at home in a neighborhood. Good websites to search: www.bnbfinder.com and www.breadandbreakfast.com. City Lights New York (www.citylightsnewyork.com) is a registry of carefully selected accomodations both hosted and unhosted. Bed and Breakfast Network of New York (www.bedandbreakfastnetny.com) is a similar registry of comfortable and affordable options .

AIRPORTS

New York is served by three major airports: **John F. Kennedy International** (JFK) and **Newark International** (EWR), the two international airports, and **LaGuardia** (LGA), mostly for domestic flights. All are managed by the Port Authority of New York and New Jersey (www.panynj.gov).

John F. Kennedy Airport (tel: 718-244-4444) is located in Queens, about 15 miles (24km) southeast of midtown Manhattan. The JFK

AirTrain (www.jfkairtrain.com) is the cheapest way to get into town. It usually takes well over an hour, but operates at 5-minute intervals during peak times (4am–7.30am and 3pm–8.30pm); every 10 minutes during non-peak hours. Take the AirTrain to Howard Beach or Jamaica stations ($5) where you can connect with A or E subway trains ($2.25) or the Long Island Rail Road (LIRR) to Penn Station. A taxi between the airport and any destination below 96th Street in Manhattan takes about 45 minutes to an hour, depending on traffic and costs $45 flat rate, not including tolls or tip. Shuttle buses cost around $15–22. SuperShuttle runs 24 hrs to any Manhattan destination and New York Airport Service runs to midtown hotels.

Newark Airport (tel: 973-961-6000) is located in New Jersey, 16 miles (26km) southwest of midtown Manhattan. Newark is usually more convenient than JFK for those staying in the Theater District. Taxis to Midtown take 30–45 minutes and metered fares usually run around $55, not including additions for tolls and crossing the state line ($10 extra) and tip. Newark Liberty Airport Express shuttle costs approximately $15 to 34th Street/Eighth Avenue, the Port Authority Bus Terminal on 42nd Street, or an east-side terminal on 41st Street (between Third and Lexington). AirTrain Newark takes you to Newark Liberty station, where you can take a NJ Transit commuter train to Penn Station (note these can be busy and are not equipped to handle large pieces of luggage). It operates every 3 minutes during peak times (5am–midnight), every 10 minutes during non-peak hours; NJ Transit commuter train schedules vary. The total cost is about $15.

LaGuardia Airport (tel: 718-533-3400) is located in Queens, 8 miles (13km) northeast of midtown Manhattan. Taxis to Midtown take 30–40 minutes depending on traffic and usually cost about $22–$28, not including tolls or tip. SuperShuttle, and New York Airport Service charge around $12–$16 for the trip. The trip by subway and bus can take considerably longer than a taxi but costs only $2.25 if you purchase a MetroCard. The M60 bus connects with the subways in Manhattan; Q33 and Q48 buses connect with the subway in Queens.

B

BUDGETING FOR YOUR TRIP

Hotel: For a double room (before tax), expect to pay over $200 per night for a budget room, up to $300 for a moderate room, up to $400 for an expensive room, and over $500 for a luxury room. The only way to spend less than $100 per night is to stay in a hostel or YMCA.
Meals: Breakfast can be had for $5; lunch costs from $6 for a sandwich and drink from a deli to $10 in an inexpensive restaurant; dinner can cost anywhere from $15 to $150 per person. A glass of wine is rarely less than $5, and a bottle is considered very cheap at $16.
Transportation: An unlimited MetroCard for one week costs $27.
Museums and attractions: Some museums and attractions are expensive ($18 for the Guggenheim), but museums belonging to the city are technically only allowed to ask for a donation, so you can pay as you wish. Many museums are free at least one evening a week.

C

CAR RENTAL/HIRE *(See also Driving)*

Since New York City has the highest car rental and parking rates in the US (as much as $80 per day), we don't recommend that you rent a car unless you plan to leave the city proper. If you do need a car, though, you'll find that it's generally cheaper to rent one at the airport than in Manhattan, and it's cheaper still to rent a car outside of New York City, where prices are more competitive. We strongly recommend that you make your reservation for car rental before you leave home. (Unusually, weekend rentals in Manhattan are more expensive than weekday rentals since most New Yorkers do not own cars and must rent when they go away for the weekend.)

You will need a major credit card to rent a car (or you must be willing to put up a very hefty cash deposit). The minimum age for renting a car is 21, but some companies will not rent to drivers

under 25, or when they do will impose a high additional fee. Rental from JFK is approximately $60-$100/day. You will probably end up paying more in parking fees than rental costs.
Avis (www.avis.com) 800-230-4898
Budget (www.budget.com) 800-527-0700
Hertz (www.hertz.com) 800-654-3131
National (www.nationalcar.com) 877-222-9058

CLIMATE

Summers (mid-June to early September) in New York are hot and humid; winters (mid-November to early March) are generally cold. Spring (early April to mid-June) and fall (mid-September to mid-November) have the best weather. While the average low temperature in January is around -4°C, it can be as low as -15°C. The wind is a major factor in how cold it feels when you are walking in the city. In summer it can get very humid with extremes at close to 38°C. Here are monthly average maximum and minimum daytime temperatures:

	J	F	M	A	M	J	J	A	S	O	N	D
°F	38	40	48	61	71	81	85	83	77	67	54	41
	26	27	34	44	53	63	68	66	60	51	41	30
°C	3	4	9	16	22	27	29	28	25	19	12	6
	-3	-3	1	7	12	17	20	19	15	10	5	-1

CLOTHING

Casual dress is fine for most places in New York, including restaurants and the theater. Only a very few restaurants strictly enforce jacket and tie policies. In the summer, light clothing made of natural fibers is recommended because of the heat and humidity. In winter, hats and gloves will go a long way to keeping the wind and cold at bay. Make sure to bring layers to cope with both the very cold and more moderate days.

CRIME AND SAFETY *(See also EMERGENCIES)*

While New York is the safest major city in the US, petty theft is still common, especially pick-pocketing at crowded intersections and subway train entrances. If you are robbed, report it to the police (tel: 646-610-5000 or 311 for non-emergencies; 911 for emergencies): your insurance company will need to see a copy of the police report (as may your consulate if your passport is stolen).

D

DRIVING *(See also CAR RENTAL/HIRE)*

Driving conditions. Visitors arriving by car would do well to leave their vehicle parked in a garage and use public transportation, as traffic and scarce parking space make driving a nightmare. If you must drive, remember certain rules: the speed limit is 30mph (50km/h) unless otherwise indicated; you may not (legally) use your horn in the city; the use of seat belts is mandatory; the speed limit on most highways in the city is 55mph (90km/h) and strictly enforced – look for signs, as on some major highways it has been raised to 65mph (105km/h); and, of course, visitors must remember to drive on the right. Before leaving home, determine whether your own insurance will cover you when you're driving a rented car.

Parking. While street parking is possible in some areas outside of Midtown, a garage or parking lot is the safer though far more expensive choice. If you find a parking spot, obey parking regulations, which may include parking only on one side of the street on alternate days (call 311 for more information). Never park next to a fire hydrant and don't leave your car over the time limit, or it may be towed away.

Gas (petrol). Service stations are few and far between in the city (Eleventh and Twelfth avenues on the West Side are good hunting grounds). They are often open in the evening and on Sundays.

Breakdowns and insurance. The Automobile Club of New York (ACNY), a branch of the American Automobile Association (AAA), will help members as well as foreign visitors affiliated with other recognized automobile associations. In case of a breakdown, or for other problems along the way, call their Emergency Road Service (tel: 800-222-4357) or wait until a police car comes along.

Automobile Club of New York: Broadway and 62nd Street, New York, NY 10023, tel: 212-586-1166; <www.aaany.com>.

E

ELECTRICITY

110-volt 60-cycle AC is standard throughout the US. Plugs are the flat, parallel two-pronged variety. Foreign visitors without dual-voltage appliances will need a transformer and adapter plug.

EMBASSIES AND CONSULATES

Embassies are located in Washington, DC, but most countries have consulates or missions to the United Nations in New York.

Australia: Consulate General, 150 East 42nd Street, tel: 212-351-6500
Canada: 1251 Avenue of the Americas, tel: 212-596-1628
Ireland: 345 Park Avenue, tel: 212-319-2555
New Zealand: 222 E. 41st Street, tel: 212-832-4038
South Africa: 333 E. 38th Street, tel: 212-213-4880
UK: 845 Third Avenue, tel: 212-745-0200

EMERGENCIES *(See also HEALTH & MEDICAL CARE and POLICE)*

All-purpose emergency number: 911

G

GAY AND LESBIAN TRAVELERS

New York has a sizable gay and lesbian population. While Greenwich Village, especially Christopher Street, is still a center for gay life (you'll find The Monster and other bars here), Chelsea is now the more fashionable gay neighborhood, where many gay restaurants and shops can be found (especially along Eighth Avenue from 14th to 23rd streets). For gay events and nightlife information, consult *Time Out New York*. Publications include *Gay City News* (http://gaycitynews.com), a newspaper covering local, national and international news and events; *HX: Homo Xtra* (www.hx.com), a gay lifestyle magazine with good events listings; and *New York Blade* (http://theblade.net) with news for the gay and lesbian community. Gay and Lesbian Hotline tel: 212-989-0999. Lesbian, Gay, Bisexual and Transgender Community Center tel: 212-620-7310;

GETTING THERE

By air. Flying to New York is a fairly simple proposition. Most airlines have several flights a day to one of New York's airports. Newark is a major hub for Continental Airlines; from Australia and New Zealand, it is served by Qantas and United; from Europe by British Airways, American, and Virgin Atlantic; and from Canada by Air Canada. Other airlines with flights into Newark include American, Delta, and Northwest; many have international connections. JFK is a major hub for Air France, American, British Airways, and Virgin Atlantic; connections to any European airline are quite good, as are connections to Canada via Air Canada, and other carriers, and to Asia and the Pacific via Cathay Pacific. LaGuardia, which serves mostly domestic flights, is a major hub of USAir, Delta, and American; Continental and United also use LaGuardia, as does Air Canada.

GUIDES AND TOURS

A good way to get started in New York is to take advantage of one of the double-decker hop-on-hop-off bus tours. For those visitors who don't want to deal with New York's transit system on their own, these are an ideal option. One choice is **Gray Line** (terminal at 777 Eighth Avenue between 47th and 48th streets, tel: 212-445-0848; www.newyorksightseeing.com).

Numerous companies offer a variety of themed tours. Cyclists should contact **Central Park Bicycle Tours**, tel: 212-541-8759; www.centralparkbiketour.com). Go in search of Edgar Allan Poe and his ghostly friends in a walking tour of East Village with **Ghosts of New York** (tel: 718-591-4741; www.ghostsofny.com). **Harlem Heritage Tours** (104 Malcolm X Boulevard, tel: 212-280-7888; www.harlemheritage.com) provides an insider's view of Harlem, and with **Harlem Spirituals** (690 Eighth Avenue, tel: 212-391-0900; www.harlemspirituals.com) you can join jazz and gospel tours. The **Municipal Art Society** (457 Madison Avenue, tel: 212-439-1049; www.mas.org) puts on history and architecture tours, while nature tours in city parks can be undertaken with **Urban Park Rangers** (tel: 311; for Central Park tours, tel: 212-360-2726; www.central parknyc.org). Finally there's the **Wall Street Walking Tour** (tel: 212-606-4064; www.downtownny.com) that takes place every Thursday and Saturday at noon (90-minute tour, free).

H

HEALTH AND MEDICAL CARE

The US has a very good though expensive health-care system, and New York has many of the country's top hospitals. Payment for any medical services will be expected on the spot. Arrange for health insurance before your visit. In an emergency, your hotel should be able to provide a list of doctors. Tap water is perfectly safe in New York.

Pharmacies. Many medicines you can buy over the counter in other countries require a prescription in the US, which must be obtained from a local physician. There are many pharmacies in New York that are open 24 hours including the following:

CVS, 630 Lexington Avenue at 53rd Street, tel: 917-369-8688

CVS, 1 Columbus Place (between 9th Avenue and 58th Street), tel: 212-245-0636

Walgreen's 212-677-0054; 145 Fourth Avenue (at 14th Street)

L

LOST PROPERTY

Each transport system maintains its own lost property office. Here are two useful numbers: **New York City Transit Authority** (NYCTA, subway network and bus system) Lost Property Office: tel: 212-712-4500; **NYC Taxi and Limousine Commission Lost Property**: tel: 311.

M

MAPS

Most hotels offer free maps but you can also pick them up at Official NYC Information centers and kiosks.

MEDIA

Magazines and newspapers. The city's major daily newspapers are the *Daily News*, *New York Times*, and *New York Post*. Several local weeklies, including *The New Yorker*, *New York*, and *Time Out New York* have information about goings on about town. The *Village Voice*, also weekly, is free.

Radio and television. Channel 1 on Time-Warner cable systems is a 24-hour station devoted to local news, weather, and events. There are about 50 local AM and FM radio stations in the New York area.

MONEY

Currency. Theere are 100 cents in the dollar. The coins are: 1¢ (penny), 5¢ (nickel), 10¢ (dime), 25¢ (quarter), and $1. Bank notes of $1, $5, $10, $20, $50, and $100 are common, but some places will not accept denominations over $20 unless you make a large purchase.

Exchange. Branches of the Chase Manhattan Bank, Citibank, and the bigger offices of other major banks change foreign currency. You can also exchange money at People's Foreign Exchange (60 East 42nd

Street, Lobby #16, across from Grand Central Station) which is open Saturdays and Sundays until 3pm.

Traveler's checks. It is wise to buy traveler's checks denominated in US$. Foreign currency traveler's checks must be exchanged at a bank.

ATMs. Most banks charge a small fee non-depositors to use their ATM machines.

O

OPEN HOURS

Banks: Mon–Fri 9am–3 or 4pm; many open Sat 9am–2pm. Some banks, such as Commerce Bank, are now offering longer opening hours (7.30am–8pm) and Sunday openings (11am–4pm).

Offices: 9am–5pm is the norm.

Stores: Mon–Sat 10am–6pm; some open till 7 or 8pm and on Sun.

Restaurants: Most are open until at least 11pm during the week, and until midnight or later on Friday and Saturday.

P

POLICE *(See also CRIME and EMERGENCIES)*

In an emergency, dial 911. The New York police department is highly visible. You will also see them patrolling the subway.

POST OFFICES

Post office branches are generally open weekdays 8am–5pm and on Saturday 9am–1pm. New York's General Post Office (421 Eighth Avenue, New York, NY 10001) has extended hours (Mon–Fri 7am–10pm, Sat 9am–9pm, Sun 11am–7pm). You can buy stamps at hotel reception desks, in many grocery stores, or from stamp machines, though these may cost more than at the post office. Mailboxes are painted blue.

PUBLIC HOLIDAYS

The following are national holidays in the US. In New York City, banks, offices, and some stores and museums are closed on these days:

New Year's Day	January 1
Martin Luther King, Jr. Day	Third Monday in January
President's Day	Third Monday in February
Memorial Day	Last Monday in May
Independence Day	July 4
Labor Day	First Monday in September
Columbus Day	Second Monday in October
Veterans' Day	November 11
Thanksgiving Day	Fourth Thursday in November
Christmas Day	December 25

T

TELEPHONES

The country code for the US is 1. New York has five area codes: 212 and 646 for Manhattan; 917 primarily for cell phones and pagers, but also for Manhattan; 718 and 347 for the Bronx, Queens, Brooklyn, and Staten Island. If you are calling a number outside of the area code you are in you must first dial 1 + the area code + the 7-digit number (though you will be charged only for a local call). Local calls cost 50¢ for an unlimited amount of time.

For international calls, dial 011 + the country code + the number. Newsstands and drug stores sell calling cards for long-distance calls.

In order to use a US SIM card you need to ensure your phone is unlocked and quad band. If so, you can purchase a card from any mobile phone store (which are numerous: AT&T, T-Mobile). However, this will not be a cheap option for international calls you may want to use pre-paid phone cards to call from a land line instead.

All numbers with an 800, 888, or 877 prefix are toll-free. You can dial directory assistance (411) for free from any payphone.

TIME ZONES

New York City is on Eastern Standard Time. In summer (between April and October) Daylight Saving Time is adopted, and clocks move ahead one hour. The chart shows the time in various cities in winter:

Los Angeles	**New York**	London	Paris	Sydney
9am	**noon**	5pm	6pm	4am

TIPPING

Service is never included in restaurant prices, but it is sometimes added to the bill. In restaurants and bars, tip 15–20 percent of the total bill (New Yorkers traditionally double the sales tax). In general, porters are tipped $1–2 per bag; maids $1–2 per day; cloakroom attendants and doormen who find you a taxi, $1; taxi drivers and hairdressers, 15–20 percent.

TOILETS

Clean public toilets are hard to come by in Manhattan. In general, the best facilities are those in the lobbies of major hotels or in department stores. Good bets in the Times Square area are the Marriott Marquis, and the Times Square Visitor Center; in Lower Manhattan, the Museum of the American Indian, and World Financial Center. There are also public toilets in Washington Square Park (closed at night).

TOURIST INFORMATION

NYC (www.nycgo.com) is a non-profit organization subsidized by the city's hotels and merchants. Their main Official Information Center is at 810 Seventh Avenue (52nd and 53rd streets; tel: 212-484-1222, Mon–Fri 8.30am–6pm, Sat–Sun 9am–5pm). There are additional Information Centers at **Times Square** (1560 Broadway, between 46th and 47th streets, daily 8am–8pm); the **Studio Museum in Harlem** *(see page 67)*; **City Hall Kiosk** (at the southern end of City Hall Park; Mon–Fri 9am–6pm, Sat–Sun and holidays 10am–5pm); **Federal Hall** on Wall Street (Mon–Fri 9am–5pm); and Chinatown (Triangle of Canal/Walker/Baxter Sts,daily 10am–6pm). There is also the **Times Square Alliance Visitor Information Center** (between 46th and 47th streets inside the Lanmark Embassy Movie Theater; Mon–Fri 9am–7pm, Sat–Sun 8am–8pm).

TRANSPORTATION *(See also AIRPORTS)*

Virtually every place that visitors are likely to go can be reached by public transportation. The flat fare is $2.25 (for bus or subway) one-way. If you purchase a **MetroCard**, you can transfer between buses and subways for free. In addition to paying for each ride, you may buy an unlimited daily ($8.25) or weekly ($27) MetroCard. MetroCards can be purchased at all subway stations and at many drug and grocery stores and newsstands, including some supermarkets. Bus and subway maps are available at major subway stations and transit hubs. For directions to reach any address in New York City by public transportation, tel: 718-330-1234. See also www.mta.info or www.hopstop.com.

Buses. All public buses are numbered and for Manhattan bear the prefix M (Q for Queens, B for Brooklyn, and Bx for the Bronx). Most either follow the avenues (except Park Avenue) or run crosstown along the major two-way arteries. They accept only exact fare (or a MetroCard). Bus stops are indicated by a signpost showing a blue-and-white bus logo, and the bus number.

Subway. It runs 24 hours a day, but not all entrances and token booths are open at all times. You may wish to avoid peak times (7–9.30am and 4.30–7pm). It is generally possible to make free transfers from one subway line to another at major transfer points. Local trains make every stop on the line; express trains do not. Lines are color-coded and identified by the last station on the line. Ensure you know the direction you're traveling in: *downtown* is southwards, *uptown* northwards. Despite occasional incidents, the subway is very safe: 8.5 million New

Yorkers ride it every day, and on many lines in Manhattan, you'll see as many people on the train at 2am as you will at 2pm.

Commuter rail lines. The Long Island Railroad provides rail service from Penn Station at 33rd Street and Seventh Avenue between Manhattan and Long Island (tel: 516-822 LIRR in Long Island and 718-217 LIRR in New York City). The Metro-North commuter railroad provides rail service between Manhattan and counties to the north of New York, including southwest Connecticut (tel: 800-METRO-INFO outside NYC and 212-532-4900 within NYC). PATH trains go from 33rd Street and Sixth Avenue to New Jersey (fare is $1.75).

Taxis. Taxis are painted yellow and metered. If the light on top is lit, the cab is available. In Manhattan you can easily hail a taxi on the street, or go to a major hotel's taxi stand. Every taxi driver is expected to be able to speak English and to be able to take you to any address in New York City; they cannot legally refuse a fare if you are going to a destination within the city limits. The meter starts at $2.50 and increases by 40¢ every ⅕-mile (or 40¢ for waiting time). There is a 50¢ surcharge 8pm–6am. There is a surcharge of $1 for peak hours (4–8pm weekdays). If your route comprises a toll tunnel or bridge, you must pay the toll. Taxi drivers will not accept bills higher than $20 and they generally expect a tip (about 15–20 percent or round up to the nearest dollar). They now accept credit cards for all fares. To complain about a driver, note his or her name and number and call 311. Such complaints are taken seriously.

TRAVELERS WITH DISABILITIES

Most New York street corners are graded for wheelchairs. Buses can accommodate wheelchairs, though many subway stations are not accessible. Many hotels have rooms for guests with disabilities, but check when you make your reservation because some older establishments do not. The Mayor's Office for People with Disabilities (110 Gold Street, 2nd Floor, New York, NY 10038, tel: 212-788-2830) can provide further details.

V

VISAS AND ENTRY REQUIREMENTS *(See also AIRPORTS)*

Canadians traveling by air must present a valid passport for entry. Visitors from the UK, Australia, New Zealand, and Ireland qualify for the visa waiver program, and therefore do not need a visa for stays of less than 90 days, as long as they have a valid ten-year machine-readable passport and a return ticket. However, they must apply online for authorization at least 72 hours before traveling at https://esta.cbp.dhs.gov. Citizens of South Africa need a visa. All foreign visitors have their two index fingers scanned and a digital photograph taken at the port of entry. The process takes only 10–15 seconds.

W

WEBSITES

The following websites will help you plan your trip:
www.newyork.citysearch.com CitySearch
www.nycgo.com Official NYC Information Center
www.timeoutnewyork.com events, bar and restaurant listings
www.mta.info regional transportation options
www.nyc.gov New York City Government's website

Y

YOUTH HOSTELS AND YMCAS *(See also ACCOMMODATIONS)*

The Hostelling International New York City Hostel is located at 891 Amsterdam Avenue, NYC 10025 (tel: 212-932-2300; www.hihostels.com). There are also two YMCAs, where you can have a single or shared room with access to shared baths on a sex-segregated floor with exercise facilities: the Vanderbilt YMCA, 224 East 47th Street, NYC 10017 (tel: 212-912-2500); and the West Side YMCA, 5 West 63rd Street, NYC 10023 (tel: 212-875-4100; www.ymcanyc.org).

Recommended Hotels

The only way to beat New York's notoriously high hotel rates is to come during the off-season (roughly between January and March) or to get a package deal or weekend special. Advance reservations are essential most of the year. You'll find the highest concentration of hotels in Midtown, between 42nd and 59th streets; others are in the 30s, both on the west side (near Herald Square) and on the east side (Murray Hill, including Gramercy Park). What you will not find here are most of the $500-plus luxury hotels, as these are out of the reach of most people.

Inquire direct about weekend specials; otherwise there are several US reservation services offering discounts of 50 percent or more on upscale rooms. Try the online service at: www.hoteldiscount.com.

The following categories apply to the cost of a standard or superior double room for one night and do not include tax of 14.25 percent plus $3.50 per room. Unless otherwise indicated, rooms have private baths, direct-dial phones, cable television, and air-conditioning.

$$$$$	over $500
$$$$	$400–500
$$$	$300–400
$$	$200–300
$	below $200

MIDTOWN

The Benjamin $$$–$$$$ *125 East 50th Street (at Lexington Avenue) NYC 10022, tel: 212-715-2500 or 1866-222-2365; fax: 212-715-2525; www.thebenjamin.com.* One of New York City's boutique-style hotels, the Benjamin offers business and leisure travelers four-star amenities and some of the most comfortable beds in New York, at relatively reasonable prices. Rooms have galley or full kitchens, and some have terraces. There is also a spa, fitness center, restaurant, and cocktail lounge. The lovely Art Deco building was erected in 1927, the work of world-renowned architect Emery Roth. 209 rooms.

Casablanca Hotel $$$ *147 West 43rd Street (6th Avenue and Broadway), NYC 10036, tel: 212-869-1212 or 888-922-7225; fax: 212-391-7585; www.casablancahotel.com.* Wonderful, small hotels are rare in New York, yet here is a lovely and inviting choice. The décor throughout evokes Morocco, with Murano glass hallway sconces and beautifully tiled and appointed bathrooms. Continental breakfast included. 48 rooms.

Four Seasons Hotel New York $$$$$ *57 East 57th Street (Park and Madison avenues), NYC 10022, tel: 212-758-5700 or 800-819-5053; fax: 212-758-5711; www.fourseasons.com.* Arguably New York's best hotel, the Four Seasons has some of the largest rooms in the city (along with some of the highest prices). Elegant features include blond wood furnishings, bedside controls for everything, and separate showers and tubs. The lobby bar is also top-notch. 364 rooms.

Hotel Edison $–$$ *228 West 47th Street (Broadway and 8th Avenue), NYC 10036, tel: 212-840-5000 or 800-637-7070; fax: 212-596-6868; www.edisonhotelnyc.com.* Hotels in the bottom price ranges hardly ever really stand out here, but the Edison is an exception. Though the Art Deco lobby can be chaotic, the rooms in this huge hotel are quite comfortable, pleasantly if simply decorated, and quiet. May be the best deal in NYC. 800 rooms.

Hotel Iroquois $$$$ *49 West 44th Street (5th and 6th avenues), NYC 10036, tel: 212-840-3080 or 800-332-7220; fax: 212-398-1754; www.iroquoisny.com.* This luxurious boutique hotel is close enough to the theater district to be convenient but far enough away to be out of the path of most of the crowds. Standard rooms are not large, but they accommodate a king-size bed without feeling too cramped. The health club is first-rate. 114 rooms.

Mansfield $$–$$$ *12 West 44th Street (5th and 6th avenues), NYC 10036, tel: 212-277-8700 or 800-255-5167; fax: 212-764-4477; www.mansfieldhotel.com.* A carefully restored Edwardian gem, the Mansfield is situated off the crush of Times Square. The only drawback is that standard rooms are small and lack real closets. Suites, however, are sumptuous. The lobby bar is a great place for a quiet drink. 126 rooms.

Millennium Broadway $$$–$$$$ *145 West 44th Street (6th Avenue and Broadway), NYC 10036, tel: 212-768-4400 or 800-622-5569; fax: 212-768-0847; www.millenniumhotels.com.* All of the rooms in this modern neoclassic tower are large and tastefully appointed, and all feature the usual business hotel amenities (two-line phones with dataports, desks, and, in Club Rooms, fax machines). 750 rooms; 125 premier rooms; 11 suites.

Paramount Hotel $$$–$$$$ *235 West 46th Street (8th Avenue and Broadway), NYC 10036, tel: 212-764-5500 or 866-760-3174; fax: 212-354-5237; www.nycparamount.com.* Designed by Philippe Starck, style oozes from every black-clad pore of this Theater District hotel just steps from Times Square, but some of the rooms are so small you feel you have to take a deep breath to turn around. On the plus side there is a good health club. 601 rooms.

The Pod Hotel $–$$ *230 East 51st Street, NYC 10022, tel: 212-355-0300 or 800-742-5945; fax: 212-755-5029; www.thepodhotel.com.* Formerly the Pickwick Arms, this recently renovated hotel will appeal to visitors on a budget looking for style and a dock for their iPod. Rooms with bunk beds start at under $100 per night in low season. Rooms with a shared bath have in-room displays to indicate the availability of shared bathrooms. 350 rooms, including 156 with bunk beds and 64 with shared bath.

Portland Square Hotel $–$$ *132 West 47th Street (6th and 7th avenues), NYC 10036, tel: 212-382-0600 or 800-388-8988; fax: 212-382-0684; www.portlandsquarehotel.com.* This budget hotel is a sister property of the Herald Square Hotel *(see page 129)*. Rooms are not large, and service and amenities are minimal, but for the price, this isn't a bad choice. 150 rooms, some with shared bathrooms.

The Roosevelt $$$–$$$$ *Madison Avenue (at 45th Street), NYC 10017, tel: 212-661-9600 or 888-833-3969; fax: 212-885-6161; www.therooseverlthotel.com.* This large hotel near Grand Central

Terminal has recently been massively renovated. Rooms are traditionally decorated. Popular with tour groups, it's a good base from which to explore the city if you don't want to be in the Times Square area. 1,015 rooms.

The Shoreham $$$–$$$$ *33 West 55th Street (5th and 6th avenues), NYC 10019, tel: 212-247-6700 or 800-553-3347; fax: 212-765-9741; www.shorehamhotel.com.* On a quiet residential street just around the corner from the Museum of Modern Art, this boutique hotel has a sleek, stylish lobby and bar. Rooms are fairly small but sumptuous and comfortable. 177 rooms.

HERALD SQ, MURRAY HILL, GRAMERCY PARK

Affinia Shelburne $$–$$$ *303 Lexington Avenue (at 37th Street), NYC 10016, tel: 212-689-5200 or 866-246-2203; fax: 212-779-7068; www.affinia.com.* Recently renovated in an eclectic, contemporary decor, the Shelburne, a member of the Affinia group, offers good-sized suites some with stunning views. Many suites have modern sleek kitchenettes and sofabeds. A good choice for families and business travelers. Order a room service hamburger from Rare Bar and Grill downstairs. Fitness center. 268 rooms. Other Affinia hotels in New York include Affinia Dumont (150 East 34th Street, tel: 212-481-7600; fax: 212-889-8856) with full service spa and fitness center.

Hotel Bedford $$ *118 East 40th Street (Park and Lexington avenues), NYC 10016, tel: 212-697-4800 or 800-221-6881; fax: 212-697-1093; www.bedfordhotel.com.* What sets this unpretentious hotel apart are its friendly staff and personalized service. The rooms and public areas are well-kept. Located on a quiet block near Grand Central Terminal. 136 rooms.

The Chelsea Hotel $$–$$$ *222 West 23rd Street, NYC 10010, tel: 212-243 3700, fax: 212-675 5531; www.hotelchelsea.com.* The Chelsea is a red-brick, Victorian landmark of bohemian decadence, home to beatnik poets, then Warhol drag queens, then Sid Vicious, and now… some of the above, plus 'ordinary' guests. For some, a stay at the Chelsea can be part of a ritual pilgrimage to all that is hip Downtown, as redolent with arty history as West Village streets and Lower East Side clubs. Accommodation varies from a few inexpensive 'student rooms' to suites, with the price mirroring the standard of the amenity. Long-stay discounts may be available; enquire.

Deauville Hotel $–$$ *103 East 29th Street (Park and Lexington avenues), NYC 10016, tel: 212-683-0990 or 800-333-8843; fax: 212-689-5921; www.hoteldeauville.com.* This inexpensive hotel is popular with budget travelers (small rooms with shared bath go for as little as $89), but it's a good location for anyone looking for a clean and simple room. The attractive building was recently remodeled, and the friendly staff make you feel right at home. 54 rooms.

Gershwin $–$$ *7 East 27th Street (5th and Madison avenues), NYC 10016, tel: 212-545-8000; fax: 212-684-5546; www.gershwinhotel.com.* A fun, youth-oriented budget hotel and youth hostel, where rooms and hallways feature the work of contemporary artists. 'Superior' rooms are spare but stylishly decorated and not too small; expect less in 'standard' and 'economy'. 150 rooms and suites.

Herald Square Hotel $–$$ *19 West 31st Street (5th Avenue and Broadway), NYC 10001, tel: 212-279-4017 or 800-727-1888; fax: 212-643-9208; www.heraldsquarehotel.com.* The former *Life* magazine headquarters is now a budget hotel popular with international travelers. While some of the rooms are dark, they're not too small (except for the singles) and are decently furnished and clean. 100 rooms.

Hotel Metro $$–$$$ *45 West 35th Street (5th and 6th avenues), NYC 10001, tel: 212-947-2500; fax: 212-279-1310; www.hotelmetronyc.com.* The lovely Art Deco lobby, with fresh flowers and leather chairs, is an oasis from gritty 35th Street. Guest rooms are fairly large and meticulously clean; the family suites are a good choice, offering two separate sleeping areas for less than the price of two rooms. Great value. 179 rooms.

Ramada Inn Eastside $$–$$$ *161 Lexington Avenue (at 30th Street), NYC 10016, tel: 212-545-1800 or 800-272-6232; fax: 212-*

679-9146; www.ramada.com. Reasonable prices and nice rooms make this small Murray Hill hotel, which has recently been fully renovated, a real find. Good Indian restaurants nearby on Lexington Avenue. Continental breakfast included. 101 rooms.

Hotel Roger Williams $$$$–$$$$$ *131 Madison Avenue (at 31st Street), NYC 10016, tel: 212-448-7000 or 888-448-7788; fax: 212-448-7007; www.hotelrogerwilliams.com.* This boutique hotel near Madison Square Park and the Flatiron Building, with a soaring lobby and soothing rooms, appeals to travelers who look for style with their room. A recent redesign of all the nice-sized guest rooms makes for a relaxing stay and an attractive choice in Murray Hill. Many rooms offer views of the Empire State Building and all feature wall-mounted flat screen televisions. Continental breakfast included with some packages. 193 rooms.

W New York: The Court $$$$–$$$$$ *130 East 39th Street (at Lexington Avenue), NYC 10016, tel: 212-685-1100; fax: 212-889-0287 or 888-625-5144; www.starwoodhotels.com.* One of the newest in Starwood's chain of high-tech, upscale business hotels, the Court has never looked better. The large rooms have all the trimmings you would expect at these prices, including Web TV and internet access with a cordless keyboard. 155 rooms, 43 suites. A few doors down, W New York: The Tuscany (120 East 39th Street, tel: 212-686-1600; fax: 212-779-7822), has 113 slightly larger rooms and 7 suites at higher prices.

Hotel Wolcott $–$$ *4 West 31st Street (5th Avenue and Broadway), NYC 10001, tel: 212-268-2900; fax: 212-563-0096; www.wolcott.com.* The gilded (though faded) lobby in this reasonably priced hotel is an attractive holdover from the Edith Wharton age. A standout in its price category. Rooms come with either one, two, or three beds and are well-kept and clean. Small fitness center. 170 rooms.

DOWNTOWN

Best Western Seaport Inn $$–$$$ *33 Peck Slip, NYC 10038, tel: 212-766-6600 or 800 HOTEL-NY; fax: 212-766-6615; www.*

seaportinn.com. A block from South Street Seaport, this converted 19th-century warehouse features antiques and more modern amenitites like VCRs and mini-fridges. Some rooms on the upper floors have Jacuzzis and/or terraces with views of the Brooklyn Bridge. 72 rooms.

Holiday Inn Downtown $$–$$$ *138 Lafayette Street, NYC 10013, tel: 212-966-8898; fax: 212-941-5832; www.hidowntown-nyc.com*. This remodeled period hotel is only a block from Chinatown and very convenient to the galleries and shops of Soho. The rooms aren't terribly large, but the hotel does offer the usual Holiday Inn amenities, and that's not a bad thing at all. 227 rooms.

Mercer Hotel $$$$$ *147 Mercer Street, NYC 10013, tel: 212-966-6060; fax: 212-965-3838; www.mercerhotel.com*. A converted 1890s landmark building right in the heart of Soho, the rooms feature high loft ceilings, arched windows, and (for New York) spacious bath facilities. Expect a stylish clientele and great food from the acclaimed Mercer Kitchen restaurant. 75 rooms.

Soho Grand Hotel $$$$–$$$$$ *310 West Broadway, NYC 10013, tel: 212-965-3000; fax: 212-965-3200; www.sohogrand.com*. A sophisticated but comfortable hotel with all the high-tech and stylish amenties you might expect from an upscale hostelry that caters to the media and music-biz crowds. As befits a place owned by the heir to the Hartz Mountain pet empire, pets are welcome; for anyone who arrives without an animal companion, the management may be able to provide a complimentary bowl of goldfish. 363 rooms.

Washington Square Hotel $$ *103 Waverly Place (MacDougal Street and 6th Avenue), NYC 10011, tel: 212-777-9515 or 800-222-0418; fax: 212-979-8373; www.washingtonsquarehotel.com*. This small, century-old, Art Deco hotel in Greenwich Village is one of the very few inexpensive options available downtown. Guest rooms, some of which look out over the park, are brightly decorated, and the restaurant, North Square, is one of the neighborhood's hidden secrets. 160 rooms.

THE UPPER EAST SIDE

The Franklin $$$–$$$$ *164 East 87th Street (3rd and Lexington avenues), NYC 10128, tel: 369-1000 or 800-607-4009; fax: 212-369-8000; www.franklinhotel.com.* The old-fashioned exterior of the Franklin doesn't prepare you for the elegant and stylish modern rooms inside. Though not large, all the modern details have been well thought out, and the human scale of the place and the hotel's friendly staff are definite pluses. Convenient to the subway and Fifth Avenue museums. 49 rooms.

Hotel Wales $$$–$$$$ *1295 Madison Avenue (near 92nd Street) NYC 10128, tel: 212 876 6000 or 866 925 3746; fax: 212 860 7000; www.waleshotel.com.* The oldest operating hotel in New York is ideally situated for visiting museums on Museum Mile. The rooftop terrace offers views of the Central Park reservoir. Rooms are elegantly furnished with great attention to detail. Room service is offered by Sarabeth's *(see page 114)*. 87 rooms.

THE UPPER WEST SIDE

Hotel Beacon $$ *2130 Broadway (at 75th Street), NYC 10024, tel: 212-787-1100 or 800-572-4969; fax: 212-724-0839; www.beacon hotel.com.* An apartment building on the way to being a hotel. The good news for travelers is that a cramped New York apartment makes a spacious hotel room, and every room has either a king bed or two double beds and fully equipped kitchenettes. Convenient to the Natural History Museum and Central Park. 260 rooms.

Milburn Hotel $$ *242 West 76th Street, NYC 10023, tel: 212-362-1006 or 800-833-9622; fax: 212-721-5476; www.milburn hotel.com.* Located just off Broadway, with Central Park only steps away, the Milburn is well situated. The hotel's amenities are nothing out of the ordinary, yet they are clean, the price is good, and the staff are friendly. Close to a wide range of restaurants. Suites have kitchenettes, and you can stock up on groceries at nearby Fairway and Zabar's, grocery stores popular with local residents. 123 rooms (including 70 suites).

INDEX

Berlitz® pocket guide

New York

Eighth Edition 2010
Reprinted 2011

Written by Douglas Stallings
Revised and updated by Karen Farquhar
Principal photography: Anna Mockford and Nick Bonetti
Series Editor: Tom Stainer

Photography credits
Anna Mockford and Nick Bonnetti/Apa 19, 22, 25, 29, 30, 33, 37, 40, 44, 45, 46, 48, 50, 52, 53, 57, 59, 60, 62, 63, 64, 69, 71, 80, 87. 96, 104; Jay Fechtman 47, 75; Abe Nowitz 8, 11, 20, 26, 35, 55, 61, 65, 67, 70, 72, 73, 76, 78, 84, 89; Tony Halliday/Apa 12, 31, 32, 39, 41, 42, 43; Britta Jaschinski/Apa 94, 99, 103; Ambient Images Inc./Alamy 91; iStockphoto 81, 83, 92; Alexandra Grablewski/Photolibrary 101; John Burwell/Photolibrary 105; Bettmann/Corbis 14; Illustrated London News 17

Cover picture: 4Corners Images

Printed by CTPS-China

Contact us

At Berlitz we strive to keep our guides as accurate and up to date as possible, but if you find anything that has changed, or if you have any suggestions on ways to improve this guide, then we would be delighted to hear from you.

Berlitz Publishing, PO Box 7910,
London SE1 1WE, England.
email: berlitz@apaguide.co.uk
www.berlitzpublishing.com

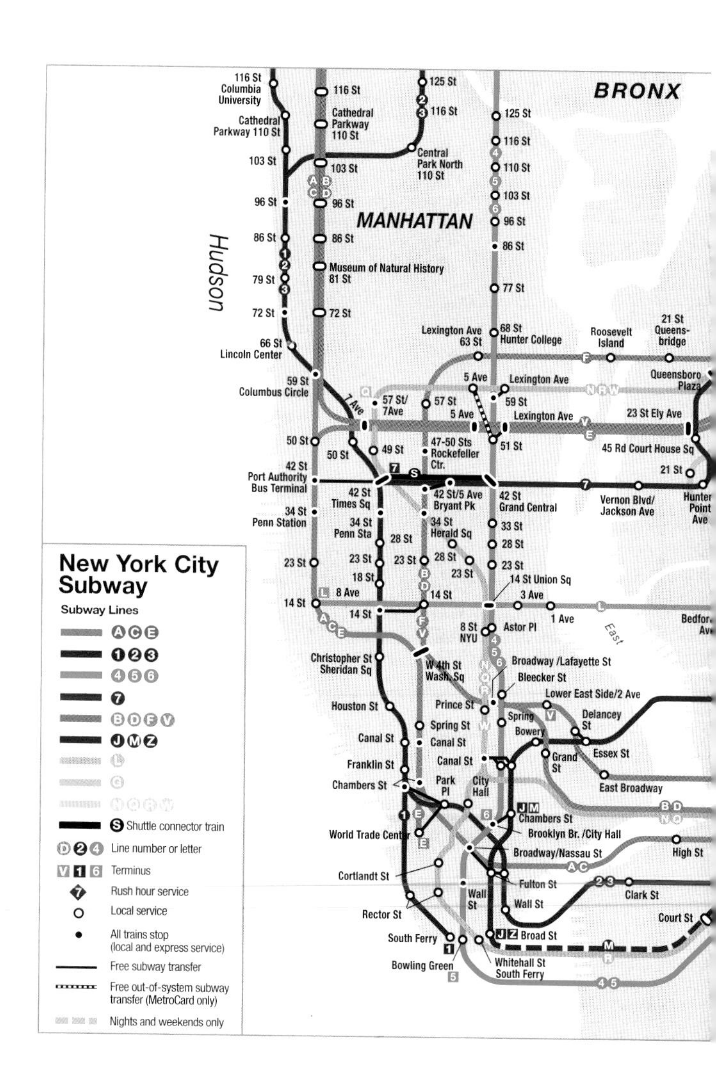

New York City Subway
Subway Lines
Shuttle connector train
Line number or letter
Terminus
Rush hour service
Local service
All trains stop (local and express service)
Free subway transfer
Free out-of-system subway transfer (MetroCard only)
Nights and weekends only
BRONX
MANHATTAN
Hudson
East

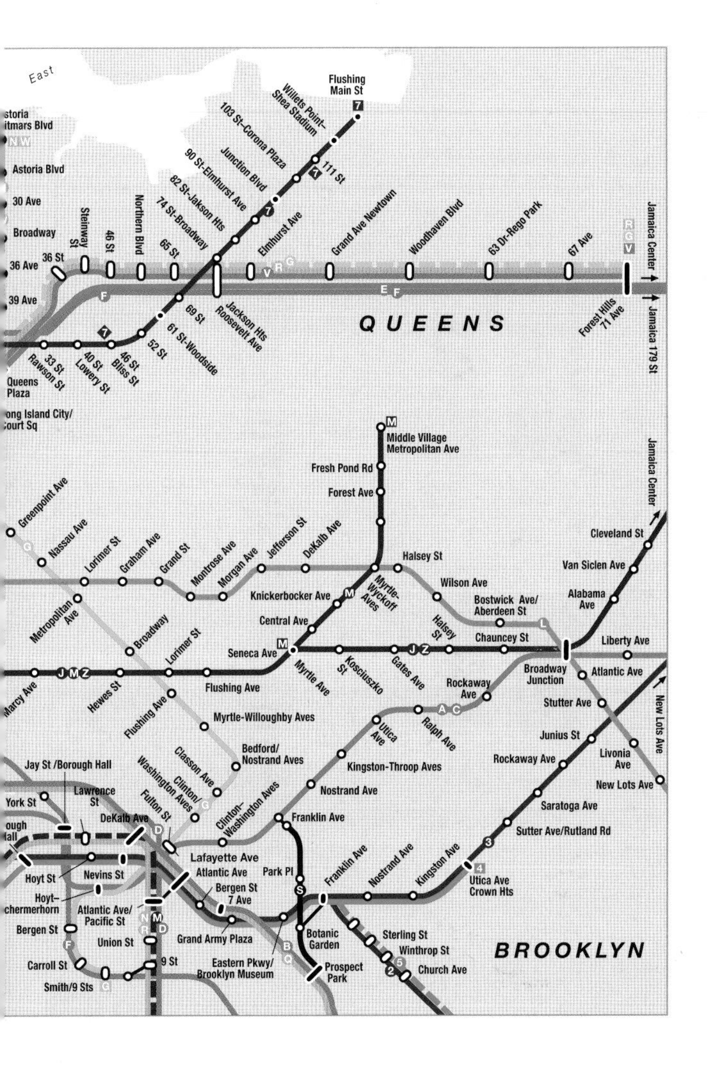

East
Flushing Main St
Willets Point–Shea Stadium
103 St–Corona Plaza
111 St
Junction Blvd
90 St-Elmhurst Ave
82 St-Jakson Hts
74 St-Broadway
Astoria Blvd
30 Ave
Broadway
36 Ave
36 St
39 Ave
Steinway St
46 St
Northern Blvd
65 St
Elmhurst Ave
Grand Ave Newtown
Woodhaven Blvd
63 Dr-Rego Park
67 Ave
Jamaica Center
69 St
Jackson Hts Roosevelt Ave
61 St-Woodside
52 St
46 St Bliss St
40 St Lowery St
33 St Rawson St
Queens Plaza
QUEENS
Forest Hills 71 Ave
Jamaica 179 St
Middle Village Metropolitan Ave
Fresh Pond Rd
Forest Ave
Jamaica Center
Greenpoint Ave
Nassau Ave
Lorimer St
Graham Ave
Grand St
Montrose Ave
Morgan Ave
Jefferson St
DeKalb Ave
Halsey St
Cleveland St
Van Siclen Ave
Wilson Ave
Alabama Ave
Knickerbocker Ave
Myrtle-Wyckoff Aves
Bostwick Ave/ Aberdeen St
Metropolitan Ave
Central Ave
Halsey St
Chauncey St
Liberty Ave
Broadway
Lorimer St
Seneca Ave
Broadway Junction
Atlantic Ave
Marcy Ave
Hewes St
Flushing Ave
Myrtle Ave
Kosciuszko St
Gates Ave
Rockaway Ave
Stutter Ave
Flushing Ave
Myrtle-Willoughby Aves
Utica Ave
Ralph Ave
Junius St
New Lots Ave
Classon Ave
Bedford/ Nostrand Aves
Kingston-Throop Aves
Rockaway Ave
Livonia Ave
Jay St /Borough Hall
Washington Aves
Clinton/
Nostrand Ave
New Lots Ave
York St
Lawrence St
Fulton St
Clinton–Washington Aves
Saratoga Ave
DeKalb Ave
Franklin Ave
Sutter Ave/Rutland Rd
Lafayette Ave
Atlantic Ave
Park Pl
Franklin Ave
Nostrand Ave
Kingston Ave
Utica Ave Crown Hts
Hoyt St
Nevins St
Bergen St
7 Ave
Hoyt–Schermerhorn
Atlantic Ave/ Pacific St
Bergen St
Union St
Grand Army Plaza
Botanic Garden
Sterling St
Winthrop St
BROOKLYN
Carroll St
9 St
Eastern Pkwy/ Brooklyn Museum
Prospect Park
Church Ave
Smith/9 Sts